QUILT OF MY LIFE'S MEMORIES

MY MOTHER'S STORY

Quilt Of My Life's Memories

My Mother's Story

By Margaret Carey

TAMARIND TREE
Toronto

Library and Archives Canada Cataloguing in Publication

Title: Quilt of my life's memories : my mother's story / by Margaret Carey.
Names: Carey, Margaret, 1948- author.
Identifiers: Canadiana 20210108991 | ISBN 9781989242032 (softcover)

Subjects: LCSH: Witecka, Krystyna, 1925-2020. | LCSH: Poland. Polskie Siły Zbrojne. Armia Krajowa. | LCSH: Poland. Polskie Siły Zbrojne—Women—Biography. | LCSH: Soldiers—Poland—Biography. | LCSH: Women soldiers—Poland—Biography. | LCSH: Political prisoners—Soviet Union—Biography. | LCSH: Women political prisoners—Soviet Union—Biography. | LCSH: World War, 1939-1945—Underground movements—Poland. | LCSH: Anti-communist movements—Poland—History—20th century. | LCGFT: Biographies.

Classification: LCC DK4420.W58 C37 2021 | DDC 943.805092—dc23

Cover background adapted from Yellow Grunge Texture Image by Beckas from DeviantArt.

This book is dedicated to my mother as well as to the memory of all the Polish Home Army soldiers who suffered and died for the country which cursed and disowned them at the time of the Communist rule.

Contents

INTRODUCTION

This is my mother's story; it is a testament to her courage, perseverance, and the belief that one must never give up.

These qualities we, her children, aspired to nurture not only in ourselves but also in our children and grandchildren.

I have tried to stay true to the story as possible while allowing myself to transcribe it in first person.

In some ways I have shared these days and nights with her.

Margaret Carey

PART ONE

M y mother was one of the most beautiful women that I had ever seen. She was tall with large robin egg blue eyes, thick dark hair which she pinned up in a figure eight at the nape of her neck, a straight small nose and a strong aristocratic chin. Her beauty was so great that a sculptor in Tbilisi, a then resort and playground of the rich and famous, expressed a wish to immortalize her in stone. The statue showing a woman with her hand on the head of a man kneeling before her was completed, the sculptor received a prize and the statue ended up in the city's museum.

Is it still there?

As this took place before World War 1 no one had returned to Tbilisi to find out.

My mother was married at the age of seventeen to a man twice her age. She bore him three children: two girls, Nina and Irene and a boy Władek*. The marriage ended suddenly when her husband died of a heart attack leaving her a young widow with a small brood.

Several years later she married a man who would become my and my older brother Wojtek's father. Her new husband was a captain in the Polish army in times when only the elite were allowed to reach the rank of officers. My father liked military order in and out of the house, and we had no choice but to fall in line and behave in a manner that was

---

*Irene and Nina perished in Auschwitz in 1944 and Władek died in a plane shot down over the Sinai Peninsula.

Libyan Arab Airlines Flight 114 (LN 114) *was a regularly scheduled flight from Tripoli to Cairo via Benghazi. An aircraft serving this flight was shot down by Israeli fighter jets in 1973.At 10:30 on 21 February 1973, the 727–224 left Tripoli, and became lost because of a combination of bad weather and equipment failure over northern Egypt around 13:44 (1:44 pm local). It entered Israeli-controlled airspace over the Sinai Peninsula, where it was intercepted by two Israeli F-4 Phantom IIs, and was shot down after refusing to cooperate. Of the 113 people on board, there were five survivors, including the co-pilot.*

worthy of children of such a disciplinarian.

I remember the more tender moments when he carried me in his arms singing softly in my ear. However, with the tenderness came the discipline. I was maybe 6 years old - I really don't remember when it started. Upon waking very early every day we had to wash from the waist up before sitting down to breakfast. The water was ice cold, but any complaints about this fell on deaf ears.

Sitting down to breakfast, lunch and dinner at the table with our parents we waited for the servants to bring our meals and, whatever was on the plates was to be eaten without negotiations, complaints or bartering. We were to learn that later in life when in social situations, this particular discipline would serve us well.

One evening, my brother Wojtek and I decided to get a jump on the misery of the early morning ritual, and before going to bed we got dressed in the next day's clothes. We even tied our shoes nice and snug to save time when the wake-up call came and the rush was on. Unfortunately, our mother came to kiss us good night and discovered our conspiracy. Back into pajamas we went. So much for that idea!

The manners we were taught were non-negotiable. When greeting our mother and father, we had to kiss their hands, then their faces. I had to curtsy and Wojtek had to shuffle his feet together and stand at attention when greeting either members of the family or guests in the house. I learned to use a fork AND knife properly at the table at the age of three and the phrase "children should be seen and not heard" was a commonly heard mantra.

I was used to playing alone. The only children that I was allowed to play with were children of other officers on occasions when there was a get-together. Otherwise, I ran in the gardens or played with my many dolls. I had twenty of them, some made of porcelain. I even had a Shirley Temple doll dressed in her typical costume. Sometimes I played with my mother, pretending that we had a store. I practiced my piano and wrote my ABC's over and over again in what I remember as a huge notebook.

When I entered grade school there was a great deal of homework to do and many books to read. I read so much that the eyes were spinning in my head, and for days I didn't want to touch a book again. Nevertheless, reading later became one of my passions.

And that was my life until my father passed away in 1936.
I was 11 years old.

•••••

As strict as my father was, so was my mother liberal.

When he fell ill and could no longer check upon us, my mother allowed me to visit a girlfriend who lived nearby. I was never able to play with her in the past because apparently, she did not belong to the "appropriate class" of people, an ideology which, as a child, I could not wrap my head around.

To me she was just another girl- a friend I could play with.

My gentle mother did not separate people into classes or colours; she treated the servants as well as the farm workers with warmth and without prejudice and often went out to chat with them when they delivered eggs, butter, and cream to the house.

One day the house was burglarized.

In spite of bars on the lower windows and bolted doors someone came in and stole several expensive items including my father's gold watch which he left on the night stand. Apparently, one of the servants let the robbers in when everyone was out for the day.

Amazingly, nothing of my mother's was touched.

The house of my childhood was located in Zielonka, a town 13 kilometers southeast of Warsaw. As there was a military range close by, a large number of officers made their home in and around the town. Sumptuous villas with massive iron gates and vast gardens dotted the landscape, and one would often spot row boats lazily traversing the small nearby lake.

Ladies colourful as Birds of Paradise, their hands lazily trailing in the water showed off their beautiful dresses while gentlemen, muscles straining in that manly show of strength rowed the boats.

In the winter once the lake froze we would don our skates and practice various spins and figure eights on the ice from dawn until dusk.

Our house was surrounded by greenery. Large, fragrant lilac bushes tightly knit together provided privacy from the street. The gardens of the house meticulously tended to by gardeners delighted the senses, as various flowers bloomed from spring to autumn. The long path in the middle of the garden was lined with irises, lilies and later with red, velvety roses. Further into the interior one could find strawberries, red currants, and several apple trees. In the rear of the garden by the fence grew raspberries with their thorny bushes which nevertheless did not deter us from picking the sweet fruit and eating it until our tummies hurt. Not too far from the house still on the property was a large gazebo covered with ivy which sheltered it from the hot summer sun.

On the other side, my father planted six linden trees, also known as Lime trees (although they have nothing to do with limes). Their heart-shaped leaves and fragrant yellow flowers always attracted bees which had us scurrying for cover whenever we heard their droning buzz.

There was a table with six chairs under the lindens. Sometimes beggars would come to the house. They were always given dinner and a thick slice of bread with butter which they ate at that table, a kind gesture of which I strongly suspected my mother.

After my father's death, my mother sent my brother and me to separate boarding schools; I went to the school run by Sisters Zmartwychstanki and Wojtek to one run by Brothers Salezjanowi.

The summer of 1939 was hot and sunny filled with carefree, lazy days. My two stepsisters came to stay with us for a little while with their children in tow, and we revelled in the closeness of the family and the beauty of the surroundings.

We had no idea that in a very short while our lives would change in a way not one of us could ever have imagined.

•••••

The town of Zielonka teemed with life as air force officers descended on it to carry out their field exercises on the nearby base.

Bringing their families with them for a few days of relaxation in the country, they were welcome guests at our house. This always kept the servants busy preparing and serving delicious meals. The house was filled with laughter and love as family banded together to drink in the lazy days of the Polish country summer-all of us blissfully unaware of a horrendous turn of events looming on the horizon.

I was three months shy of my fifteenth birthday, but I looked and acted slightly older than my calendar years. Tanned, with long brown hair plaited in thick braids I caught the eye of a young officer by the name of Waldemar who came to our house with his uncle. Soon, our mutual attraction blossomed into a fast friendship. Once a week he arrived at our house and took me for long bike rides in the country.

Waldek which is what I called him, would always stop at a nearby store to buy me chocolate gingerbread cookies and colourful jellies which I loved. We took long walks and I felt proud and adored having a handsome young officer by my side.

My sister Nina sounded alarm bells telling my mother that I was too young for a suitor, but my mother smiled and reassured her that Waldek was a very well brought up and intelligent young man and there was no harm in this summer friendship. And a friendship it was.

Waldek was very polite and never tried to kiss me or even hold my hand. Suspecting that I may be only 16, he told me that he would wait for me to grow a little older, and I was happy with that promise.

After all, we had a whole life ahead of us.

In August of that year, strange rumblings of an impending conflict began to appear in the news. There was to be a "lightning quick" war and citizens were told to store some supplies for no more than one month in case of such an event.

My mother, heeding such a warning, had the servants prepare some emergency food baskets which contained delicious wafers, jams, pates, coffee, and tea . That was all. Surely we would be well prepared for a war which was to last less than a month.

A soldier from my father's regiment came to stick crisscrossed tape on the windows of the house to prevent breakage of the glass in case of bombs landing nearby. (One never even considered a bomb landing ON the house; such was our innocence and trust in the media!)

The officers left Zielonka, and Waldek left with them.*

My oldest sister Irene came to Zielonka with her two children: Jurek who was 10 years old and Lala (nickname meaning "doll") who was 8 years old.

When the Germans crossed the border into Poland, they took her husband who was a veterinary surgeon and director of a large meat plant which produced and distributed meat products to the entire country, as a hostage.

(Our lives would not cross again until he tracked me down in Canada, but a half of a century had passed by then, and our lives had taken on entirely different paths. He wrote to me for a while and sent some lovely paintings that he had done, but we never met again. In spite of 50 years spent apart, his death left a strange and unexplained void in my life.)

He was taken to a concentration camp and shortly afterwards executed. In view of the internment of her husband, Irene and her children were now made aware of the danger they were in, so they remained in Zielonka, leaving their beautiful manor in Gdynia unoccupied.

The adults did a great job in keeping the seriousness of the situation in Warsaw from us youngsters.

We had no idea that the capital was being bombed mercilessly, and the Germans were advancing closer every day. The only thing that was odd was the occasional appearance of German bombers which, flying low would pepper the town with bullets.

Sometimes this happened when we were in the gardens. The adults taught us to run to the sheltered gazebo and lie down on the ground. We thought this to be great fun- a game of sorts, and mercifully, no one was hurt during those fly by shootings.

•••••

As weeks passed, the gravity of the situation hit us like a ton of bricks. Leaving our serene and beautiful property in Zielonka, we moved to Warsaw and into an apartment on Wielka Street.

My two sisters and their children moved to a one-bedroom apartment on Puławska Street. With all schools shut down by the Germans we studied in private homes, still believing that this situation must change, and we would be shortly returning to our daily lives.

As occupation ensconced the city, my mom, a gentle, aristocratic, and privileged woman, rolled up her sleeves and entered into conspiracy with no hesitation.

Doing nothing in these troubled times was not in her vocabulary, so she began to sell all her belongings in order for us to survive, leaving only a couple of beds and a table in the apartment. She also became active in keeping and distributing underground newspapers, storing them in the ceramic heater which stood unused due to the fact that we had no money for coal to heat our humble abode. Although, as a young woman she never needed to clean or cook, and more than that, never needed to worry about life's inevitable details, she would always joyfully announce: "we will manage, we will always manage".

Shortly, I was retained by the underground organization for an activity which I carried out without fear or trepidation for such a *laissez-faire* attitude is the privilege of youth.

Every day, after taking the streetcar to the central train station I was met by a man carrying a parcel wrapped in a special patterned paper. Upon meeting me he would utter a code phrase to which I would respond with a previously taught word.

With a firm grip on the mysterious package, I rode another streetcar, proceeded to a station at a second location where I boarded a train, and carried on to the town of Skarrzysko-Kamienne.

There, finding the designated drop-off point in an old apartment building I climbed the rickety stairs to the very top story and, with a provided key, opened the door to a tiny, empty apartment.

There I would place the mysterious package and return to Warsaw on the next train.

(The contents of those packages would remain a mystery to me forever.)

The only thing hidden in that tiny apartment was a revolver. I knew its hiding place as my orders were that in the event of being followed, I would shoot myself to avoid giving up any information to the enemy under the inevitable torture. This was understood and oddly acceptable; I knew that I would carry this out without hesitation if the need arose.

My mom was by now deeply ensconced in conspiration. As she spent a great deal of time on the telephone, she relied on her co-conspirators who worked for the phone company to alert her in the event that the phones were being tapped by the Germans.

Her colleagues would say: "that will be enough of the lentils", and she would hang up immediately. I always wondered why she always had boxes of lentils lying around the house.

Summer was quickly approaching. My two sisters moved back to Zielonka where the underground organization set up a small factory for the production of ammunition, and in which both of my sisters were very active. I continued to carry out the role of a messenger and regularly moved packages from one town to another as ordered. Such activities if discovered would be catastrophic; therefore, our daily life, which hung precariously over the ledge of death was led under the constant cloud of secrecy and vigilance.

In the heat of that summer of 1940, my mom decided to send me to a cousin's estate called "Marcinowo" located a few kilometers from

Leopoldow, and which, miraculously was still free of the German occupants.

The original estate was immense, and my grandfather's brother who was the original owner divided it into three sections-one for each of his children. The estates were in a stunningly beautiful setting, surrounded by forests and lakes full of fish. I arrived at the estate of my uncle Leon Czerniewski, and life was good once again.

We often rode in a horse drawn cabriolet or went for a horseback ride through the beautiful countryside

My uncle would take me duck hunting; it was my job to row a boat and pick up the fallen ducks to bring them home where the servants prepared them for dinner.

In spite of the circumstances in the rest of the country, Marcinowo seemed to be frozen in time. The servants still took care of the house, the cooks prepared the meals and set the table with porcelain and silver.

After dinner, young people from neighbouring estates arrived at our house and we played volleyball or other games. Sometimes we went for walks in the forests, or for a row on one of the many lakes.

On Sundays, we climbed into the cabriolet pulled by Uncle Leon's two beautiful dapple-grey horses and headed out to church, where seats were designated for the various families of the area.

In the heat of that summer, I revelled in the normalcy of life.

I will always be grateful for those few weeks in the country before my life took a sad and frightening turn.

And in the heat of that idyllic summer, away from the horror of the devastation that was taking place in the city of Warsaw, I fell in love for the first time.

His name was Kazik and he was the nephew of our parish priest, with whom he came to spend some time while temporarily escaping from the quickly advancing terror in Warsaw.

As Kazik was alone, my cousin Leon invited him to our house to meet some people his own age and enjoy a game of volleyball.

Tall, handsome with impeccable manners, his calm demeanor so diametrically opposed to my own immediately caught my attention.

The feeling must have been mutual because, after that first day his visits became frequent and regular. This resulted in complaints voiced by my cousins stating that he only had eyes for me and paid virtually no attention to any of them.

Truthfully, this suited me just fine; I was as smitten as anyone can be, especially realizing that the feeling was most certainly reciprocated.

As the halcyon days of that summer flew by, Kazik spoiled me by walking 4 kilometers from his uncle's home to ours in order to place flowers and sweet pears which I adored, at the stairs in front of my bedroom.

He then returned to his uncle's house only to come back to see me in the afternoon. We often took walks in the country, holding hands and revelling in our new and all-encompassing love.

One morning Kazik was caught by his uncle as he was getting ready to make that long trek to my house. His uncle questioned him as to where he was off to.

The first thing that came to Kazik's mind was to tell his uncle that his stomach was very upset, at which point his uncle sprang into action by giving him castor oil mixed with milk to "clean out" his digestive system.

And that it cleaned it out one must say, was an understatement.

When he finally stopped running to the bathroom he was able to come for a visit and tell me of his misadventure.

We laughed about it for a long time, although I'm sure when the castor oil was doing its job, Kazik was not much in a laughing mood!

It was only many years later that I appreciated the sacrifice my young man made in order to bring me those small gifts every morning.

One day Kazik took me to the crypt under the church of his uncle's parish. There were quite a few coffins containing the embalmed bodies of the local gentry.

As he lifted the lids I could see the bodies, gray but complete without any signs of decomposition. Strangely, we saw this bizarre setting as a museum, a place where we will all be one day.

We had neither fear nor distaste in our discovery.

Inevitably the summer came to an end and with it a time to part. Kazik took my address in Warsaw and promised to contact me when I returned there.

In the time we spent together we never talked about the Organization, although we knew that both of us were active members. The motto was that if you don't share knowledge it cannot be dragged out of you during the inevitable torture.

I suspect that down the line this gag order saved my life.

After Kazik left I fell ill with dysentery, a vicious epidemic unleashed in the vicinity which claimed the life of my 6-month-old baby cousin. Although very sick, I managed to beat this disease and left our beautiful country home to return to Warsaw where I resumed my duties as a courier for the Organization.

One day after delivering the package to the empty apartment in Skarżysko-Kamienna, I waited for the train going back to Warsaw.

To my horror, Gestapo stormed the platform and arrested everyone standing there.

Once the train arrived, they pushed me into the wagon.

The train was a Pullman with the long narrow corridor between the cabins; at the other end of the corridor, I noticed several people who were arrested and stood under the careful watch of the Gestapo.

I stood alone on the opposite side. The soldiers who shoved me onto the train remained on the platform and the train left the station.

Before we reached the city of Radom it occurred to me to check if the door through which they shoved me was locked.

No one was watching me.

The Gestapo soldiers were busy at the other end of the corridor, and the German sentry several feet away stood with his back to me.

I felt the train slowing down. Without hesitation, I pushed the handle, opened the door, and jumped out of the moving train tucking and rolling down the steep slope.

I was glad that as a young girl I learned to jump from the still-moving streetcars.

In those days, there were not enough streetcars to serve the population and you could always see people hanging from the open doors clutching handles and each other. We called these hanging bunches of people "grapes". It took some practice not only to hold on, but also to jump off when the streetcar was still moving without falling under its wheels. Failing to jump off in time you could be trampled by others trying to get off at the same time.

After I stopped rolling, I got up and began to run. I swear I had wings as I ran so fast that my feet barely touched the ground. Once I reached the shelter of some bushes and stopped running, I swept the sand and the dirt off my clothes and calmly returned to the station where I got on the next train and returned to Warsaw.

•••••

The close call with the German Gestapo on the train did not deter me from continuing my courier activities, in spite of rumours that the Germans suspected the area to which I travelled to be dangerous on account of partisan presence. Because of this, they regularly conducted raids on the trains, arresting all the passengers convinced that among them they will find the few "bandits" as we were called.

Several days after my close call, the Germans boarded the very train on which I was returning from the little apartment in Skarżysko-Kamienna to Warsaw from another delivery and arrested everybody present. They took us to a house which they occupied in the town of Radom and locked us in a room on the first floor. There was no need for sentry, as the room had bars on the windows. In their opinion, we could not go anywhere, and so they left.

Little did they know that when I began my courier activities, my mom gave me a file which I always carried in my boot. I looked around at the various frightened faces and approached a few young men to tell them about my secret possession. We organized everyone in the room to keep a watch on the door and began to sing hymns and children's songs in a very loud voice, which in turn muffled the noise of filing the thick bars on the large window.

Taking turns, we filed for what seemed hours. Thankfully, the Germans, confident that we were safely ensconced in that secured room, did not bother to return and check out what possessed us to sing our hearts out with such glee.

Eventually, we managed to cut through two bars; that was all we needed for one person at a time to be able to squeeze through. We began to jump out one by one from a height of about eight feet. I don't know how many of us managed to escape because, just like the time I jumped from the moving train I flew as fast as I could away from that house, never looking back. I swear that if I were a contestant at the Olympics that day I would have garnered a gold medal.

I ran to the train station and, to my relief a train was there ready to depart. Once again, I returned safely to Warsaw.

While I continued to carry packages between Warsaw and Skarżysko-Kamienna my two sisters Nina and Irene stayed in our beautiful home in Zielonka with their children. Without hesitation they continued to use the home as a base for ammunition storage and distribution, as well as a base for production of false documents which would save many lives down the line.

One evening a Polish spy arrived at the house accompanied by several soldiers of the Gestapo, and my two sisters as well as their three children were taken away and transported to the Pawiak prison.*

Our efforts to free my sisters turned out to be fruitless. However, with the help of my oldest brother Władek, the children were released.

My brother picked them up on the street where they were told to wait and took them immediately to our uncle's house.

Sadly, we were not able to gain the release of my sisters who were transported to Auschwitz.

Heartbroken, my mom and I moved into the small apartment which was occasionally occupied by my sisters when they were in town.

We did not stay there long, as shortly after our arrival my mom got the news that we must immediately leave Warsaw.

There was an impending raid on our home.

The home where we were to stay was already predetermined for us. Our new destination was the town of Suchedniów.

The town stood in the vicinity of the Świętokrzyskie mountains and forests which would soon become my next home.

My sister Irene's two children Jurek and Lala, as she was known, remained living with our uncle, but Nina's only child Adam, whose nickname was Dadek was to come to stay with us.

I went to the train station on the day we were told he would arrive. Quite nervous and worried that I might be observed and/or followed,

*Pawiak was a prison built in 1835 in Warsaw, Poland.
Following the German invasion of Poland in 1939 it was turned into a German Gestapo prison, and then part of the Nazi concentration-death camp system. Approximately 100,000 men and 200,000 women passed through the prison, mostly members of the Armia Krajowa, (Polish Home Army) political prisoners and civilians taken as hostages in street round-ups. An estimated 37,000 were executed and 60,000 sent to German death and concentration camps. [2] Exact numbers are unknown, as the prison's archives have never been found.

I struck up a conversation with a girl around my age, and we ended up going to her house where I could watch for the approaching train from the balcony.

Finally, the train arrived, and I ran to the platform to watch for my little cousin. He came down the steps of the train carefully, clutching a small backpack. His blue eyes, big as saucers showed all the terror and confusion that lived in his 6-year-old heart.

I grabbed him by the hand, and we ran. I was so afraid that we were being watched that I did not stop to check if anyone was following us but ran holding Adam's little hand. He could barely keep up with me but tried his very best to run without falling. We reached the town of Kleszczyny which stood on the other side of the railroad tracks; there my mom and I found a temporary shelter.

My mom was waiting for us and hugged little Adam until his heart slowed down its frightened flutter. Having travelled for miles on the train by himself he told us that all he could see while he was on the train was peoples' feet, and that he was very frightened.

He cried for a while wanting to be with his mom, not yet knowing that he would never see her again.

•••••

I had no idea that our life was in constant danger as I fearlessly carried out the duties of a messenger.

After the internment of my sisters my mother became increasingly alarmed by information received through her contacts of an impending raid on our home. This led her to contact Eugeniusz Suszyński, an aide-de-camp to the commander of the Home Army, Tadeusz "Bór" Komorowski. Through him, she got in touch with lieutenant Jerzy Stefanowski "Habdank", a commander of a detachment of "AK", (Armia Krajowa) the Polish Home Army.

The fate of my partisan life was sealed. I was sent to Wykus, a place 5 km. southwest of Starachowice in the Świętokrzyskie Mountains.

After a lengthy and uncomfortable trip, I reached a camp in the middle of the forest and the scene I came upon startled me to the core.

A group of young men stood at attention while a soldier who appeared to be a platoon leader reprimanded them in a most vocal and stern way. I had never been witness to such discipline and momentarily felt a sense of fear gripping my throat as well as a sincere wish to return to what life was left at home with my mother.

But that was army life and that was to be my new home; I had to adapt.

There were only a few tents in that forest as the base was newly formed, so I had to sleep in the communal tent with the men.

Our new home was an elongated canvas structure where we slept on a bed of boards and thin, straw mattresses, one next to the other like sardines in a can.

Sometimes the rains came down in buckets. To stay more or less dry we crawled under the boards and slept on the ground. This provided us with a somewhat acceptable place to sleep without the possibility of being soaked through and through.

Eventually, we began to build our own shelters. The boys built a luxurious accommodation for me made with thickly interlaced ever-green branches and a few sheets of canvas for the roof.

Now when it rained, all I had to do was run my fingers in a straight line along the roof of the tent and the water dripped inside along that trajectory and not on my head.

Lieutenant Habdank decided that since I was the only female in this platoon I needed direction in order to be a useful part of the group.

And so he began to teach me first aid, followed by combat arms training and maintenance of weapons. This included the detailed knowledge of firearms, including memorizing of names of each and every part, as well as disassembling and reassembling of the rifles and handguns, which included 9mm. Stens, Infantry Rifles as well as light and heavy Machine Guns. My training facility was a large bunker lo-cated by the river and recently discovered by the soldiers of my pla-toon. There I practiced shooting. Machine guns were my favorites, with their rapid discharge and solid weight.

The river next to the bunker served as our bath and I found a spot around its bend where I could bathe without any witnesses.

During the stay in the camp, our help was often called upon by the local farmers in nearby villages.

Sometimes the Germans would come into the village and select a cow to be taken away for their use. In such a case, we would come into the village at night and take the cow away. When the Germans arrived for their spoils, the villagers complained loudly that bandits came at night and stole the cow.

Satisfaction was twofold: for the villagers, because they did not serve to help the Germans and for us because we had food for another week.

Our help was also required when the villagers told us they had an informer among them who passed on information to the Germans. The solution was easy: the informer was caught and transported to the camp where he was interrogated by the Commandant. The spy then had to dig a shallow grave, and subsequently had his short career ended with a bullet to the back of the head.

Sadly, he was not the only informant whom we had to liquidate. It seems that war brought out not only the heroes but also the cowards among us. In the murderous wake of the German machine against the villagers who dared to help the partisans, was the village of Michniów, and following the horror story that was its liquidation, the partisans, under the leadership of Commandant Ponury conducted an attack on a German train.*

•••••

We were already versed in blowing up trains, as we were occasionally warned by the villagers that such a train, carrying weapons and supplies to the German troops was on its way.

The train tracks were rigged with explosives and the subsequent fireball was always satisfying.

This of course always led to a retaliation by the Germans. The battles were fierce, but our determination was even more fierce, and we

---

*During World War II, the region of Michniów was occupied by the Germans from September 1939 until January 1945. Under the occupation, it was one of the local centres of the Polish underground resistance movement. On 12–13 July 1943, a population of Michniów was massacred by the German Police units of the 17th and the 22nd Police Regiments, commanded by Hauptmann Gerulf Mayer, in punishment for the partisan activity in the area. In the first massacre, on 12 July 1943, 98 men were burned alive locked in barns. The same night, the partisans headed by Jan Piwnik "Ponury", made a retaliatory assault on a German train from Kraków to Warsaw. The Germans returned to the village the next day and committed a second punitive massacre. For a period of two days, at least 203 inhabitants were killed - 103 men, 53 women and 47 children. After ad hoc investigation, a further 11 persons - the only ones suspected by the Germans of underground activities - were sent to Auschwitz concentration camp, where 6 died. The village was then completely burned.

fought with every ounce of strength and courage we could muster. The result was a considerable number of casualties on the enemy side.

Thankfully, the Germans were not keen on entering into the forest; therefore, we could always withdraw into its heart with an illusion of safety for our lives.

•••••

In the midst of the horror and the duress that became our daily living, the character of each person became transparent.

Such was the case of a former hero of the underground, Jerzy Wojnowski with a pseudonym of "Motor"*.

Under the pretext, which was revealed later he became an informer for the Germans in order to secure a release of his mother from internment, and the price for that was to bring the German troops to our camps in the forest.

The first group hit was one led by inspector "Jacek"-Jan Kosinski.

The Germans bombed the site from the sky. Among the planes were three assault and one reconnaissance plane.

Flying low, they dropped packets of grenades and small calibre bombs while their pilots peppered the partisans with bullets from deck machine guns. The raid came just before dawn taking the life of 25 soldiers, including three young brothers.

I could not imagine the anguish of their mother when she learned of this murder.

Commandant Ponury-Nurt determined to break through the ring of the advancing enemy quickly organizing a group of stormtroopers armed with machine guns and grenades. With lightning speed, they hit the road Siekierno-Wąchock. The fierce retaliation was such a surprise to the Germans that they quickly began to retreat leaving their posts behind. This was the biggest and most painful battle for the Partisans on Wykus.

---

*MOTOR-Jerzy Wojnowski

Wojnowski was an agent of the Kielce Gestapo nicknamed "Garibaldi" - "Mercedes". The man who betrayed colleagues, became their most cruel executioner. His path to the activities of agents has never been fully explained. We do not know the exact time of obtaining it by the German Secret State Police, nor the motives that guided him. Incidentally," Motor" was also behind the raid and executions of the men, women, and children of Michnów.

33 partisans were killed and 5 were taken as prisoners of war. Those were executed, most probably somewhere in the forest. The Germans, who conducted attack on several hundred Partisans with the aid of 12,000 soldiers lost 100 of their men.

And so, our somewhat quiet nights in the primitive but relatively comfortable camp ended as we began the constant relocation, usually under the darkness of night.

I remember looking at the Big Dipper as we walked along, each person with his hand hooked under the belt of the person in front. The night was quiet, and the stars shone with ethereal beauty.

It was not unusual for us to fall asleep, exhausted but still moving forward during those walks.

And fall asleep I did. Waking up with a start, I saw a small line of my colleagues disappearing on the horizon.

I was completely alone.

Panic rose in my stomach and I ran as fast as I could until I caught up and hooked my hand under the belt of the last soldier in line.

Eventually, we reached a village and entered an old barn. The sight of the straw piled to the rafters was more magnificent than even food and water.

I fell completely spent into the fragrant straw just as I heard "Przekora, take your boots off or you won't be able to walk tomorrow". I did just that and fell into a deep and dreamless sleep.

While living in the forest, my clothing was eaten away by lice. The sweater I wore was threadbare and my underwear was now paper-thin. Only my riding breeches survived their ravenous raids.

Even though we tried to burn the lice off each other with pointy sticks dipped in the fire, we were losing to the onslaught of these nasty critters.

Washing was impossible as rivers were frozen over and the very thought of wading into what water was running free was horrifying. Therefore, used snow to clean ourselves.

Several times we had what was called "Concentration". This was a gathering of several partisan groups together to exchange intelligence, share supplies and generally decompress from the brutality of the surrounding situation. At one of these meetings, I walked into a tent of the group which we were visiting to borrow a spoon.

I almost fell over when I saw who was sitting on the boards.

It was Kazik. We had no idea that we were both fighting in the same forest, or that either of us was still alive. Our reunion was wonderful, and I heard Kazik say that this was the happiest day of his life.

But our happiness was short-lived as we both had to return to our own units at the end of this time.

In the next while, the group with which I lived began to dissipate and go into hiding as our position was no longer safe. It was time for me to go.

"Nurt" ** came to me and said: "You are one of the last people remaining here. Go to find your mom; maybe you will survive."

After such a cheerful order there was nothing for me to do but return to Warsaw. Things were fairly quiet in the city when I returned. My mother was overwhelmed with joy to have me home safe and sound, if not particularly clean or lice-free. It was a full house with my cousin Ludwig's daughters Hania and Marysia as well as my brother Wojtek and our nephew Jurek.

Christmas was approaching and Kazik came to visit filling the longing and the void in my strange life that was so full of exile, loneliness, and hardship. We went for walks on the streets of war-torn Warsaw and, as we walked, Kazik pointed out a place where violets once grew in the spring.

We walked and sang a song: "A bouquet of violets will tell all. It's wonderful to be with you. Without you the world is empty."

He brought me beautiful leather boots made by a partisan cobbler, and a bottle of perfume.

These were the most precious Christmas gifts I had ever received, and we marveled at the beauty of those moments, revelling in the warmth of each other's love and grateful for the relative peace of the season among the skeletal remains of our once beautiful city.

•••••

Days flew by as I carried out my duties for "the Organization" as we called the underground group, and Kazik and I continued to look

----

**Jan Piwnik ps. "Nurt", "Grim" (- the captain of the Polish Army and aspirant National Police, posthumously promoted to the rank of Major, and then to the rank of colonel (2012); commander of the guerrilla Army in the Holy Cross Mountains and Nowogrodek.*

forward to each and every day together as our love continued to grow and mature.

On January 28th of 1944, he told me that he was going to a meeting with Commandant Ponury-Nurt about a possible deployment out east.

He hugged me very tight and promised that he will be back in time for dinner.

The afternoon dragged on; I had a feeling of uneasiness that I could not explain. My stomach was churning, but I put it off to a rather old piece of bread I ate earlier.

Dinner time came and went and there was no sign of Kazik. Tears were welling up in my eyes and my throat tightened. Something was wrong. I could sense it.

Days went by with no sign or message. I knew that Kazik must have fallen into the enemy's trap and now I was in full panic.

One morning soon after his disappearance I received a message scribbled on a 20 złoty note with three words on it:" I'm at Pawiak".

Prisoners often threw such notes out of the window of the paddy wagon which carried them to whatever horrible destination was meant for them. The people of Warsaw knew that this was a desperate attempt to reach a loved one and would pick up the notes on the street and take them to the address scribbled on them.

In Kazik's case, the banknote was used by a German officer who paid with it for a ticket to Radom, not noticing or ignoring the address and the message written on it.

It was the teller who kept it and delivered it to my house.

I cried nonstop, wishing that I could see him gain; wishing that we could make a life together when this awful war finally ended.

I put together a package for Kazik and took it to Pawiak. They accepted it. That was a good sign-a sign that he was alive.

Two more notes followed with a brief communication. The last one, written in February was brought to me by an elderly gentleman. It read: "Go to my mom. Keep up her spirits. You and I will meet again - on the other side - with God."

He must have known that he was going to his death.

I thought that my life was also ending. I lay in bed from dawn to dusk wishing to be with him; wishing to share his pain; wishing to die with him.

Eventually, I put together another package and took it to Pawiak. This time they did not accept it, and I knew for sure what that meant.

Pawiak was known for cruelty and torture. I knew that if Kazik broke under interrogation and gave up names of the partisans we worked with, mine would have been among them, and I would have certainly been imprisoned and most likely killed.

But he did not tell them what they wanted to know, and this cost him his life.

Years after I emigrated to Canada I returned to Poland and desperately set out to find any trace of Kazik and his last hours.

Starting at Aleje Szucha*, the old quarter of the Gestapo known for its brutal interrogation and torture, I scanned the walls for any sign scribbled on them and pored over books in the cases left over from those horrendous times.

Then I went to Pawiak and searched for any sign; anything at all. But I found nothing. Where did they take him? Did he suffer? Where did he die? Where was he buried? I never found out.

The briefest time of happiness was torn out of my young life. In it there was no time to play, no time to feel free or safe, no time to believe that the future was ours to have.

The carefree moments full of love and laughter were torn from my hands with brutal finality.

But life went on and once again I was sent away; this time towards the Kampinowskie area where I shared a house with a young nurse.

The "Organization" gave me a bicycle on which I rode into different locations in order to observe the movements of the Germans, learn of any arrests and find out if spies for the enemy were among us.

In due course, I was released from my duties and allowed to return home to Warsaw.

It was August of 1944 and Warsaw was in the midst of an Uprising.** The city was in flames when I arrived and getting to my home was not even remotely possible.

---

*Aleje Szucha- Interrogations were extremely brutal. The victims were beaten with batons, whips, and sticks. They had broken bones, crushed genitals, eyes, and teeth knocked out, they were strangled, burned and flooded. Tortures took place in the interrogation room, where members of victims' families were often present.

I had to turn back. A decision that most likely saved my life.

•••••

Warsaw was on fire; it was dying a slow and certain death.

There was no choice for me but to leave. I climbed into a wagon of a freight train carrying coal and covered in black coal dust arrived in the city of Łowicz where I made my way to the R.G.O.

This was a bureau of organized help which provided shelter, clothing, and food for any of the Polish citizens who found themselves homeless and penniless. I was able to have a bath and change into clean clothes donated to the cause.

Shortly after my arrival, I saw a woman appear at the shelter. She walked in, or rather sailed in with her cape unfurled and revealing her corpulent countenance. On her face was a look of determination, and by her side sailed a mirror image of her in a mini size, which I determined had to be her daughter.

The larger of the two inquired, in a voice as determined as her entrance: "Is there anything for me?"

Baffled by this question, I strained my ears to hear the answer.

"Yes. Three youngsters," came the reply.

Jesus, Mary, and Joseph! The blood ran cold in my veins. She is involved in human trafficking. I'm done for.

Mercifully, it was explained to me that this woman, a baroness no less, took displaced Warsaw citizens into her estate and provided them with temporary shelter.

A kind, generous soul. Sadly, I don't remember her name or even the name of the town she lived in. Only that it was close to Łowicz.

When we arrived at the estate, we were fed and given a room to sleep in. We also had to dig a trench outside in the garden. This served us well as I found out in a few days.

**The Warsaw Uprising was a major World War II operation by the Polish resistance Home Army to liberate Warsaw from Nazi Germany. The Uprising was timed to coincide with the Soviet Union's Red Army approaching the eastern suburbs of the city and the retreat of German forces. However, the Soviet advance stopped short, enabling the Germans to regroup and demolish the city while defeating the Polish resistance, which fought for 63 days with little outside support. The Uprising was the largest single military effort taken by any European resistance movement during World War II.

I was picking and eating the sweet summer strawberries in the yard when I heard the Baroness call "Malaika", as that was what she called me.

A Malay girl. Did I look Malaysian with my tanned face and broad cheek bones? I don't know. I never questioned her choice of names for me.

"Malaika", she called, "into the trench! The Germans are coming!". I jumped in and she covered the trench with pine tree branches, and quiet as a church mouse waited until the danger passed.

I don't know how many people this noble woman helped, but her deceit was never uncovered by the enemy. May the Good Lord reward her for her generous heart.

I knew I couldn't stay in this paradise forever, so I prepared for the road by visiting a nearby cobbler. I asked him if I could use his tools to fix my boots which were now falling apart. I remember the beautiful boots Kazik brought for me what seemed a lifetime ago. Sadly, I had to leave them behind in Warsaw and now they were gone forever.

I sewed the holes in my boots covering them in cloth and returned to the estate to thank the Baroness for her help, and for the wonderful couple of weeks I was able to spend in relative safety.

And so, I continued my exile.

I grew hungry as the day progressed. Crossing a field, I noticed carrots growing and pulled one out to satisfy my hunger. Immediately, a peasant ran out from a nearby hut, and shaking his fists at me called me a thief and a bandit. So much for human kindness.

However, the elusive kindness returned in a few days.

I was walking through a small village when a woman called to me and asked where I was from.

When I told her that I was from Warsaw, she called me to her and brought a good-sized piece of bread and a pair of clean under panties.

I know it sounds bizarre, this combination of gifts, but a million złotys could not make me happier than these two things.

I thanked her warmly and headed down to the river. There I took off my well worn out panties, washed them and hung them on a branch to dry. Weariness overcame me; I climbed under some tree branches and fell into a deep and dreamless sleep.

Alas, upon waking I noticed that my now clean panties were gone.

Apparently, some passerby needed a pair of used panties and decided to make them her own.

But that was war time in which rules and borders of decent behaviour were blurred. It was a time of the honorable and the dishonorable. A time of executioners and the executed. A time of hunters and the hunted, and the time of the righteous and the deceivers.

I would, at some time or other, come upon all of these.

•••••

It was time to move on toward Koziṅskie.

I knew that the "Organization" was posted in that town, but what was more important to me was the fact that Kazik's mother lived there and, as strange as this idea seemed I felt that I could vicariously reconnect with the man I loved.

I walked for miles, sometimes picked up by a kind soul in a horse-drawn carriage or in a truck carrying who knows what.

When I finally reached the town, I found Kazik's home, knocked on the door with my heart in my throat and introduced myself to his mother. She greeted me warmly, gave me a bed to sleep in and fed me soup to fill my empty stomach.

It took me a few days to regain my strength and get some much-needed sleep, this time in a real bed and not on the ground or in a ditch hidden under branches.

Sadly, I decided to leave Kazik's mom's place after she began to worry about her safety which could result in more arrests and perhaps executions of the members of her family, a family which was already in the bull's eye for conspiratorial activities.

She was justified in her worry; Her son-in-law and her only son Kazik were arrested and executed for their activities in the organization, and now her safety was compromised by my presence.

I thanked her and, with the help of the local farmers found another house where I could put down some tentative and temporary roots. It was time to contact the Organization.

After an interview, I was given a bicycle and began to work again.

The jobs included the delivery of various papers and packages as well as tracking and reporting any spies in the area who would subsequently be brought into the woods and executed.

Polish women who took up with the German soldiers were whipped and had their heads shaved to serve as a warning to the rest of the female population on the area.

1944 was coming to an end and under the attack of the Russian army, the Germans began to retreat often bringing roads to a standstill because of sheer numbers of their vehicles packed with fleeing soldiers.

While I worked in Kozińskie, my mother, who had my little orphaned nephew Adam in her care, unbeknown to me was taken by the Germans along with hundreds of other Warsaw citizens for transport to a concentration camp.

The freight train was packed, shoulder to shoulder with people. It was hard to breathe and there was no place to sit or lie down. My mother knew that they would not survive this horror.

At one point the train stopped to let a few people out in order to allow them to relieve themselves in the field. My mother begged the guard to let her take little Adam for the same reason.

The Germans were under great stress to get this transport out as soon as possible before the Russians would stop them, and did not pay a great deal of attention when the people were herded back into the train, thus offering my mother the opportunity to slip quietly into the woods holding fast onto the hand of her little grandson.

The decision most probably saved both of their lives.

When the train departed, my mom began the long walk to Grójec where Princess Lubomirska dedicated several buildings on her property as a shelter for any Polish citizens who needed a temporary roof over their heads.

In the meantime, I was very fortunate to establish contact with my brother-in-law who was in a prisoner of war camp*. It was through him that I was able to find out where my mother was, as she was also in contact with him.

Relieved and ecstatic that I found out she was still alive, I decided to set out, once again to join her and little Adam in the shelter in Grójec.

The German army vehicles were beating a hasty retreat from the rapidly encroaching Russian troops. They did not care when Polish

---

*Prisoner of war camps. The Germans established several camps for prisoners of war (POWs) in territory which before 1939 had been part of Poland. ... The POW camp in Grądy (Stalag 324) held 100,000 Soviet prisoners; 80,000 of them perished.

people would jump onto their vehicles in order to catch a ride in whatever direction they needed to go. Far too fixated on their own escape they ceased to care about these hitchhikers, of which I was one.

Jumping from one German truck onto another, I was able to cover quite a lot of ground in my desire to reconnect with my mother and my little nephew.

Suddenly, I found myself in the middle of a Russian ambush. There was no retreat for the Germans as the Russians were already pulling up in the rear.

Now the Russian tanks and vehicles stood on each side of the road and when a German truck neared it was peppered with machine-gun fire or hit with a flamethrower. There was no escape nor was there time to introduce myself as a Polish citizen.

I watched as the vehicles ahead of us were picked off like sitting ducks. The only saving grace was that the Russians had to reload, so one vehicle would be able to pass and escape while the one that followed exploded in a ball of fire as it was hit.

Hair stood up on my head and fear gripped my throat as I counted the cars. That one was hit, the next one passed through. Was ours the lucky one, or were these my last moments on earth?

I decided to seek higher power.

"Dear God," I prayed. "Please spare this car and I promise that I will get off this truck and I will walk the next 300 kilometers that are left of my journey."

We drew closer; the car in front of us exploded, hit by a mortar. We were safely through. But as a recipient of human weakness, after I thanked God for sparing my life, I said meekly: "Dear God, please let me ride a bit longer on this truck. Please don't be angry with me. I'm all alone and it is so far to travel."

I think I heard Him laughing.

•••••

I stayed on the truck heading towards the town in which I believed my mother found shelter. Exhausted by lack of sleep, fear of losing my life and the constant, gnawing hunger in my belly I nodded off until we reached the barracks which housed refugees from Warsaw.

Among them, in one of the barracks I found my mother and my little orphaned cousin, little Adam.

The barrack housed 16 people, each of whom had some kind of im-
provised bedding spread out on the floor.

"Where do you sleep?" I asked her.

She showed me a small area where she lay her old fur stole that she
wisely kept with her. This now served as a bed for Dadek. She slept on
the floor next to him.

Seeing my mom sleeping like a beggar, tears welled up in my eyes
and, in spite of my wish not to cry escaped down my cheeks. My mom
took me in my arms and comforted me, telling me that this situation
was only temporary and that we would get through it very soon. I
know that she had no idea if and when these horrible circumstances
would come to an end but seeing me so distraught she mustered up all
her courage to appear positive and cheerful.

I had to leave my mom to return to Końskie and garner my small
military allowance. With the money received, I bought some material.
There I asked Kazik's sister who was a seamstress to sew some stockings and underwear for my mom and for Adam.

The Germans had deserted the town of Końskie leaving everything
behind, including identification documents of the Polish citizens sent
to Siberia to fight the advancing Russians. Now the Organization set
out to save the lives of these people who would be in the crosshairs of
the Russians for their so called "volunteered" aid to the German cause.

We had to act quickly in organizing help. The documents and clothing that we managed to collect were hidden behind a panel in the ceiling, and each person who came to us was given a document with a
picture that most resembled him or her. The new identity would save
their lives.

Their military uniforms were burned and replaced with civilian
clothing. They could now move more freely around the country, seek-
ing members of their family who were still alive.

It was midnight, January 8th,1945 when we were surprised by a visit
from the NKVD, a Russian version of the German Gestapo.

Several soldiers came in and began to make sarcastic comments
about needing some clothing, but their humour did not last long.

They told me to get ready to go with them and followed me into
the next room where I told them I would get my coat. While they were
busy supervising me, the men escaped quietly through the front door

leaving me to my fate. I was taken to the local NKVD headquarters and what happened next tested my resilience to the core.

Placed in front of the wall in the courtyard I realized that I was going to be executed.

The soldier aimed and placed his finger on the trigger. At that point someone called him away, and I was left standing there, shivering in the cold.

He returned and the scenario was repeated.

This went on for a period of time which I cannot even recall, but I am sure it was a good part of the night.

Staring down the barrel of the rifle I wondered if this time he will pull the trigger, because if this was to be I wanted to turn my head away. I obsessed about being shot in the face. Death was O.K.; dying by a bullet to the face was not. Such stupid thoughts whirled about in my head in the moments I believed to be my last on earth.

Their psychological game was played out in order to break me; they wanted information on who, what, where and when with regard to the distribution of passports and aid to the Polish soldiers.

But in spite of the all-night mock execution, I would not be broken.

I reeled with exhaustion, along with my young executioner who nevertheless never pulled the trigger.

With the arrival of dawn, we were both trying not to fall asleep.

Seeing him swaying as he sat on the bench I offered to hold his weapon so he could have a nap.

Bleary eyed, he extended his rifle to me and caught himself at the last minute.

"Oh no, you don't," he said in Russian, "you will shoot me".

Brilliant, to say the least.

In the morning, my execution was clearly stayed as I was now herded towards one of a long columns of trucks preparing to transport a considerable number of people to Siberia. I was one of them.

The column of trucks was long, stretching as far as the eye can see. Exhausted and hungry, I watched a few trucks in front continuing their journey eastward as our truck and several others came to a stop.

In no time at all we were taken off the trucks and put up in small huts under the watchful eyes of our captors.

I soon found myself alone in an empty room.

Isolated and devoid of any human contact I wondered what fate awaited me at the hands of these barbarians.

I needed to use the toilet.

A Russian soldier was my escort and standing next to me pointing a gun at my head waited until I finished my business. To this day I can see his large boots as I squatted to pee in the primitive outhouse.

On the third day of this strange internment, I was taken to another house two doors down. One NKVD interrogator began the process of trying to break me down with questions as two others looked on. The interrogation went something like this:

"Where do you live?"

"I'm from Warsaw."

"What was your role in the organization?"

"I want to go home."

"If you cooperate with us, you will have a good life."

"I want to go home."

"We know that you were involved in falsification of passports and aid to deserters."

"I want to go home."

"We want you to work with us. If you become a spy for us, every luxury will be yours."

"I want to go home."

The Russian's face took on an unhealthy red tone and he leaned over me. His small eyes bugged out his head as he whispered: "You will not get away with this. Have a nice life in Siberia."

Two soldiers were summoned to take me away, and to my surprise, I recognized the Russian soldier who came to us as a spy, and whose uniform I burnt before I handed him a falsified passport.

Our eyes met briefly; I saw a mockery in his half-smile as he pointed towards a column of pick up trucks filled with people and ready for departure. "Get going" he snarled. Pushing me towards the door he walked quickly to his waiting car which then drove to the front of the already moving row of trucks.

I froze stunned at finding myself alone and unsupervised in the hallway of the house. I realized he was confident that I would do what he ordered me to do, which was to board one of the trucks; it never occurred to him that I would have the guts to disobey his orders surely risking my life. I flattened myself against the wall holding my breath, watching the unfolding scene through a crack in the door.

The Russians were busy pushing people onto the trucks. Not as organized as the Germans, they had no clue that one of those people was missing and huddling behind a closed door a few feet away.

Finally, the trucks began to pull away. As the last one disappeared on the horizon, I burst out of the house and headed in the direction opposite to the one chosen by the trucks.

I had no idea where I was going, but one thing I knew for sure: I wasn't going to Siberia.

As the houses we were brought to were at the far end of town I found myself running towards a field.

The sight I came upon was shocking: snow-covered roads were strewn with bodies of German and Russian soldiers.

Legs, arms, glassy eyes staring at the gray skies, bloody uniforms staining the snow, backpacks still intact painted a macabre scene in the shrill silence of the freezing dusk.

I spotted a white jumpsuit in one of those backpacks and gingerly removed it; these served as camouflage for the German soldiers in the snow-covered fields.

This one would provide some warmth and protection from the elements in my journey to…I really didn't know where.

•••••

I started to walk quickly through the open, snow-covered fields, still terrified of being found.

My punishment would surely be a bullet to the head.

As dusk descended I spotted a rickety wooden barn and cold, hungry but most of all exhausted to the point of falling I snuck in through the propped-up door.

The barn was empty except for a few burlap bags and a rafter filled with hay. It was an easy climb.

Reaching the fragrant bed, I crawled like a field mouse under the hay and covered myself as much as I could with an empty burlap bag soon falling into a deep and dreamless sleep.

Awaking at dawn, I climbed down and with bits of straw sticking out of my hair began to walk briskly towards the unknown.

I alternately walked and ran in order not to freeze to death should

I stop and rest in the snow-covered fields. As hours passed, frost made itself at home on my hair, eyebrows, and lashes.

Many years later, as I watched the film Dr. Zhivago, it all came back to me; I looked and felt like he did in those hostile fields that almost rendered me snow blind.

The hunger and thirst began to overtake me. To my delight, I spotted a hut in the distance and reaching it I gently knocked on the door.

A peasant woman of about 50 plus years opened the door slightly.

As I asked if I could get a drink of water she began to scream and point towards the fields with her crooked, dirty finger, waving me away. I didn't understand her language; It sounded like Ukrainian.

Having no choice but to keep on walking in any direction, I gathered up my strength and began a journey to who knows where.

Walking through the bare, deserted fields I only stopped to cup a handful of snow in my hands and eating it, thus quenched my insistent thirst.

Throughout this journey the landscape changed, but only marginally.

At times, the fields were bordered by thick forests; at other times frozen, stiff bodies lay twisted into various macabre poses in the shrill silence of the barren landscape.

The day was winding down and dusk began to cast shadows on the snow. In the distance, I saw a road; beyond It as far as the eye could see, loomed a dark endless forest.

Something inside me broke and a gripping fear clutched my throat. Three days and two nights of this lonely, hungry pilgrimage to what I could only hope would be a safe haven now called a halt to the next impending challenge.

A wolf howled in the darkness and I began to shiver with fright.

My feet were suddenly made of lead, refusing me another step. My throat tightened and tears rolled down my cheeks, freezing halfway down as I wept.

Alone, hunted, forgotten, cold, tired, and hungry, for a moment I wanted to lie down in the field beside one of those frozen bodies and sleep. Sleep without a wish of waking up again.

Another wolf howled and a pack joined in. It was both beautiful and frightening, but the wolf calls snapped me out of the self-pity which covered me from head to foot.

I shook off the lethargy and began to pray. "Dear God," I pleaded "please help me; let me find some people, let me find a shelter. Even if it is Moscow ahead, I don't care. Please help me."

Suddenly, a truck appeared in the distance. Elated at the sight of any civilization, I raised my hand to stop it.

The truck filled with Russian soldiers passed by without even slowing down.

A second truck approached. I waved, but it kept on going. Then a third. It also continued on its way passing me by with indifference.

I raised both hands and with tears streaming down my cheeks and cried towards the heavens

"God, can you hear me? I will surely die in this wilderness. I am afraid to continue through these forests."

Suddenly I heard a motor behind me; a truck stopped a few feet away and a Russian soldier jumped down and walked towards me.

"Where are you going?" he asked in Russian.

"I am running away. I was taken prisoner by the Germans," I replied in my halting Russian. It was the only thing that would save me. Should they find out that I was a Russian prisoner, my life would be over.

"Please take me with you," I begged.

I didn't ask where he was going; I didn't care where he was going. Confusion swirled in my head, and all I could think of was that I just wanted to be with people and away from this crushing, murderous solitude. He looked at me intently for a minute or so, finally saying "get on the truck."

That was all I needed to hear. Jumping up with what was left of my strength I soon fell into a deep exhausted sleep.

After about 6 hours I awoke, but the truck continued on its way without stopping. We drove for another 4 hours or so until we came to a small town. The Russian nudged me saying: "Get off now."

Finding myself on the deserted street, fear came back with a vengeance. This was the 6th year of living under occupation, always with the knowledge that one can be arrested and/ or killed any minute.

First, by the Germans, now by the Russians; both evil and merciless.

The arrests, exiles, and killings continued.

Our fight for freedom rang hollow and defeated. We were a nation of hostages now, and the world looked on in silence.

There wasn't a living soul on the street where I stood. This was "police hour" or a curfew during which no one was allowed to be on the street. It was enforced from 8:00pm to 6:00am every day.

I flattened myself against a wall in the arch of a building and looking at my surroundings I reeled in shock. I was in the same place in Końskie from which they took me for transport to Siberia.

•••••

I walked into the apartment housing the small office of the Polish Home Army and to my surprise, came upon a group of my colleagues with whom I fought in the forests.

"Where did you come from?" they shouted, running to hug me.

"Directly from the gates of hell," I replied. "But God allowed me to escape."

My head was swimming and my legs buckled under me. I couldn't remember when I last ate but the crushing weariness finally overwhelmed me and, knowing that I was safe here, I lay down on one of the beds in a nearby bedroom and fell into an exhausted sleep.

My respite, however, was short lived. The commandants of the Polish Home Army gave us orders to disperse. We had to leave our temporary home and return to whatever place we could still call home.

I managed to find a freight train carrying ammunition which was heading to Warsaw.

It was scheduled to leave at 4:00am but, as it was the only game in town I could not be picky, so I climbed aboard and settled on top of the tightly packed ammunition. I had all my earthly belongings with me: a small package with some clean clothes given to me by my friends at the apartment, a couple slices of bread and a small purse in which I carried a picture of my father in his military uniform.

The Russian soldiers marched up and down the corridors, guarding the ammunition. They didn't bother with me; it was not unusual for civilians to climb aboard and catch a ride to wherever they were heading.

Soon I fell asleep, rocked by the rhythm of the rails.

When I awoke, my package and my purse were gone. Only a slice of bread which I kept in my pocket remained intact.

But such was the nature of our "Liberators".

The train finally came to a stop.

I was in Warsaw, my home. But Warsaw was now a field of charred ruins as far as the eye could see.

Occasionally one could spot houses still standing, but that was a ruse as mines were placed around them in readiness for their destruction.* I tried to orientate myself but to no avail.

Winter held the dying city in its grip. Rats scurried across my path, running in and out of the skeletons of burnt out buildings. No streetcars, no stores, no lights or even trees remained in this apocalyptic landscape. Bodies of men, women and children lay everywhere in the silence of this forgotten city of the dead.

As I walked along the now non-existent streets I saw people coming out of the ground. Those were the basement dwellers living in all that remained after the city was levelled. ** At last, I found our apartment; amazingly, it stood proudly among the ruins. On its door hung a sign "House Demined". It was safe to enter. I knocked on the door and to my delight my mom stood before me. My mother, thin and tired, but whole and safe, threw her arms around me and we wept together with the grief of our broken lives, our lost loved ones, our destroyed homes but also with the happiness of being together and of survival in spite of such terrible odds.

"Mama, did you eat? "I asked her. "No, not for about a week now," she replied.

I took out the piece of bread which I managed to keep in my pocket

---

*Special groups of German engineers were dispatched throughout the city in order to burn and demolish the remaining buildings. According to German plans, after the war Warsaw was to be turned into nothing more than a military transit station. The demolition squads used flamethrowers and explosives to methodically destroy house after house. They paid special attention to historical monuments, the Polish national archives, and other places of interest whose destruction was carried out under the supervision of German scholars. What couldn't be taken by Germans was to be burnt or destroyed. Nothing was to be left of what used to be the city of Warsaw. Ref. Wikipedia.

**Some people hid in the deserted city. They were called "Robinson Crusoes of Warsaw" or cavemen. Germans called them rats and killed them if they were found within the city ruins. The best-known Warsaw "Robinson" was Wladyslaw Szpilman. Szpilman's experiences were adapted in the film The Pianist.

and offered it to her, but she declined saying that I should eat it. Yes, my insides were twisting with the gnawing hunger, but I would not let her know that. I told her that I had a second piece of bread which I ate just before finding her and I wasn't hungry. Only then did she agree to take the bread from me.

It was time to search for some food in the basements of the city.

This was not a pleasant task for many reasons, one of which was the presence of huge rats which claimed the city as their kingdom.

For a few moments, I entertained the idea of killing a rat for dinner but their size, (that of a small dog) deterred me from approaching them. I feared that I might become their dinner instead.

In one of the basements, I found a bucket which once held molasses. Scraping the sides with my fingernails, I managed to get some of the sickly-sweet tar-like treat and sucked it off my fingers. The taste was so horrible that I instantly felt nauseous and abandoned the idea. To this day I cannot stand the sight or smell of molasses.

I kept the bucket, however. That was a commodity which would come in very handy when I returned home.

There was a pond behind our apartment building which had the poetic name of "The Eye of the Sea".

The only thing that resembled the eye of anything was that it was round. One had to conquer a steep decline in order to reach the pond, but we were desperate for water so down I went carrying my newly acquired bucket.

There were quite a few of us with the same idea so, in the spirit of helping each other we joined hands allowing the person closest to the water to fill their bucket and be pulled up onto the level ground.

When it was my turn I filled my bucket and safely brought it home.

It was hard not to notice that the water had a terrible stench; people said it should be boiled three times before consumption, but I thought nothing of it. Plugging my nose, I drank it from the bucket. Thirst won over. After the war, the area around the pond was made into a park and the pond was cleaned.

The surprise find was bodies of three German soldiers which, decaying in its depths contributed to the terrible smell.

How I didn't get deathly ill, I'll never know.

•••••

The small apartment in which I found my mom living had a ceramic heater which extended from the floor to the ceiling as well as a wood burning stove which graced the kitchen. Unfortunately, we did not have coal necessary to heat our rooms nor wood to be able to cook a meal on the stove.

I had no choice but to go out and search for something with which to make a fire.

A Russian sentry stood by a nearby tree talking to a man with a large black dog on a leash. Behind him lay a long tree branch.

With my heart in my throat, I approached the guard from behind and, as stealthily as I could grabbed the large piece of wood and slowly started to drag it away. The Russian burst out laughing startling me and I almost dropped it, but he kept on talking and laughing with his friend never noticing me and my haul.

The dog however, observed my movements and wagged his tail in glee.

Some watch dog, I thought, but I thanked him in my heart for not alerting his master to the strange young girl with a tree branch which, by the way, looked like a big dog toy.

My heart was pounding in my chest and I was sure that I would be caught, but I remembered our freezing apartment and continued to softly drag my burden away from the two men and towards the apartment building where we were now housed.

A problem remained however and it was how we were going to cut up this branch.

Off I went again - this time I descended into the building's cellar where once the caretakers kept their tools for various repairs and emergencies.

Miraculously, I came upon a small hatchet and, armed with my treasure ran upstairs to begin cutting up the wood for use in the two stoves.

We were doing well: we had wood for heat and water in the bathtub for cooking. We had a candle which I also found in the cellar and a box of matches kindly given to me by a neighbour who was also living in the remains of what was our building.

Our apartment was completely empty except for two beds if you could call them that, as they were only frames with springs. The mattresses were missing.

We had neither a table nor chairs.

Over the course of the war the Germans pillaged belongings with unending enthusiasm.

What they left behind was stolen by our own thieving citizens for their own use.

The devastation of war brought out the worst in some people. Mercifully, it also brought out the best in others who banded together to support each other in those dark and uncertain times.

I lit a candle in the darkness of our cold apartment and suddenly there was a knock on the door, or rather on the frame of the door.

The middle of the door was cut out by thieves but my mom patched it with a piece of drywall she found, and it served its purpose in the best way it could.

The knock on the door startled and unnerved us. My mom, pretending that there was a man living with us called out: "Richard, somebody's at the door!"

The danger of two women being found alone was great as being raped by Russian soldiers was rampant and common.

"For heaven's sake Richard," my mother cried, "hurry up! Stop dawdling. Oh OK, I'll get it!"

"Anybody there? Open up, if you are you alive." Male voices exclaimed on the other side of the door. "We are Polish soldiers."

My mom slowly opened the door and four strapping young men in uniform entered.

"How are you surviving? Do you have any food?" they asked.

There were no stores, no one had money, lives were torn apart and survivors were living in conditions that could only be described as inhumane.

The only food we had in the past two weeks was some wheat that my mom found. She cooked it turning it into a tasteless mushy mess and I had to eat it very slowly because it was so disgusting that with every bite I had the urge to vomit.

The soldiers told us that they will be going to the outskirts of Warsaw where the farmers were baking bread, and they will bring us a couple of loaves. We agreed that they will knock three times and say a password we decided on. They were true to their word and the next day they came back with two freshly baked loaves of bread.

My mom took one, I took the other, and we sat on the floor biting and tearing into the fragrant loaves blessing the soldiers for their kindness.

That was the best loaf of bread I ever had. I will never forget how good it tasted, how good it smelled, how it felt in my hands as my hunger was slowly satiated.

In my life, the gift of that delicious bread went down as one of the most precious and wonderful days of my life.

The soldiers did not forget about us and from that day on they brought soup from the military base in their canteens. I thank God for the care and the giving spirit of the people who looked after the ones who were in need.

In the worst of times, we found the best of times.

And among the worst and hateful people we found the best and loving ones.

I will never forget them.

PART TWO

Rosary And Black Bread

A story of one woman's courage in the face of evil

FOREWORD

This is the story of my mother's internment by the NKVD* and UB** of Post War Communist Poland, as translated from her memoirs.

As a member of the Polish Home Army, she was one of the many Polish soldiers persecuted by the Communists after the war. This eventually led to her decision to leave Poland and start a new life in Canada.

This story is a testament to her courage, perseverance, and the belief that one must never give up; qualities which we, her children aspire to nurture not only in ourselves but also in our children and grandchildren.

I have tried to stay as true to the story as possible while allowing myself to transcribe it in first person.

In some way I have shared those days and nights with her.

I dedicate this book to my mom as well as to the memory of all the Polish Home Army soldiers who suffered and died for the country which cursed and disowned them at the time of the Communist rule.

The People's Commissariat for Internal Affairs. The agency was originally tasked with conducting regular police work and overseeing the country's prisons and labor camps.

**The Ministry of Public Security (Polish: Ministerstwo Bezpieczeństwa Publicznego), commonly known as UB or later SB, was the secret police, intelligence and counter-espionage agency operating in Polish People's Republic, which closely resembled the East German Stasi and Soviet KGB. From 1945 to 1954 it was known as the Department of Security (UB), and from 1956 to 1990 as the Security Service (SB).*

THE POLISH HOME ARMY
(POST WAR)

The Home Army was officially disbanded on 19 January 1945 to avoid civil war and armed conflict with the Soviets.[1] However, many former Home Army units decided to continue operations.

The Soviet Union, and the Polish Communist Government that it controlled, viewed the underground, still loyal to the Polish Government-in-Exile, as a force to be extirpated before they could gain complete control of Poland.

Future Secretary General of the Polish United Workers' Party, Władysław Gomułka, is quoted as saying: "Soldiers of the AK are a hostile element which must be removed without mercy." Another prominent Polish communist, Roman Zambrowski, said that the Home Army had to be "exterminated."[2]

By war's end, some 60,000 Home Army soldiers had been arrested, 50,000 of whom were deported to Soviet Gulags and prisons; most of these soldiers had been taken captive by the Soviets during, or in the aftermath of, Operation Tempest, when many Home Army units tried to work together with the Soviets in a nationwide uprising against the Germans.[2]

A major victory for the Soviet NKVD and the newly created Polish secret police, Urząd Bezpieczeństwa (UB), came in the second half of 1945, when they managed to convince several Home Army and WiN leaders that they truly wanted to offer amnesty to Home Army members.

Over a few months they gained information about great numbers of Home Army and WiN people and resources. By the time the (imprisoned) Home Army and WiN leaders realized their mistake, the organizations had been crippled, with thousands of their members arrested.[2]

The persecution of the Home Army was only part of the Stalinist repressions in Poland. In the period 1944–56, some 2 million people were arrested,[2] over 20,000 were executed or murdered in communist prisons,[2] and 6 million Polish citizens (every third adult Pole) were classified as "reactionary" or "criminal elements" and subjected to spying by state agencies.[2]

Most Home Army soldiers were captured by the NKVD or by Poland's UB political police. They were interrogated and imprisoned on various charges such as "fascism".[3][4] Many were sent to Gulags, executed or "disappeared."[3] Thus, between 1944 and 1956 all the members of Batalion Zośka, which had fought in the Warsaw Uprising, were locked up in communist prisons.[5] In 1956 an amnesty released 35,000 former Home Army soldiers from prisons: some had spent over 10 years imprisoned for the crime of fighting for their country.

---

1. *Sabotaż i dywersja, Bellona, London 1949, vol.1, p.21; Article on the pages of the London Branch of the Polish Home Army Ex-Servicemen Association. Retrieved 14 March 2008.*

2. *Wielkie polowanie: Prześladowania akowców w Polsce Ludowej (Great hunt: the persecutions of AK soldiers Andrzej Paczkowski. Poland, the "Enemy Nation," pp. 372–375, in Black Book of Communism.*

3. *Crimes, Terror, Repression. Harvard University Press, London. Retrieved 7 June 2006.*

4. *Michał Zając, Warsaw Uprising: 5 pm, 1 August 1944, Retrieved on 4 July 2007.*

5. *Żołnierze Batalionu Armii Krajowej "Zośka" represjonowani w latach 1944–1956," Instytut Pamięci Narodowej, Warszawa 2008, ISBN 978-83-60464-92-2*

CHAPTER I

January 22nd, 1951

I remember the date well. It was 22nd of January, 1951.

There were only the three of us living in the tiny two room apartment on Puławska Street: my mother, my one-and-a-half-year-old daughter and me.

The apartment building was one of the few still miraculously standing after the horror of the war. Most of Warsaw was slowly getting up off its knees to begin the rebuilding of what was once a vibrant and lively city. The living room window looked over a small courtyard with an even smaller patch of grass. The window of the only bedroom looked over the street with its shops and streetcars which clanged and rang their warnings well into the night.

The memory of war was deeply etched in our hearts. It was an integral part of our family history as both my mother and I worked relentlessly to save ourselves and others through those dark years.

Our stately home in Zielonka, a town just outside of Warsaw became a hub of conspiratory activity with the collection, storage and distribution of arms and the falsifying of passports that would save many lives. It was also an established meeting place for leaders and partisans who would carry out the resistance in the face of overwhelming odds.

We would pay a great price for such behaviour.

In 1942, a Polish spy infiltrated our operation and brought the information back to the German headquarters.

My two sisters, Janina and Irena were the only ones home on the day the Germans came to the house. They were shipped out to Auschwitz.

I will never forget the day when a letter arrived in the mail. It was sent on 30th of December 1944 and its message was short:

"We wish to inform you that Irena Bartnik, prisoner #53851 died on March 2nd, 1944. Janina Wieczorek, prisoner #53897 died on March 3rd, 1944."

My mother's face is etched in my memory for all eternity. At first, disbelieving, it turned into a mask of unbridled grief as she sank to her knees.

The first sob, guttural and primitive turned to a scream.

"You are murderers! Murderers! You killed my children!" She wailed between sobs.

"Mama, stop. Please be quiet. They will kill us," I pleaded.

The German post was only a few yards away, and I knew that if they hear us, they will kill us as surely as we were standing there.

It was after that day my mother contacted a friend of hers, a commandant in the underground army of partisans known as The Polish Home Army, and my fate was sealed. For my own protection, I would go to the forest and join the partisans. I was only to live with them, not to become one.

That, however, was not an option for me, and soon I learned to take apart and clean a rifle and ultimately, to use it.

So, on that day, 22nd of January 1951, I had returned from work as an office clerk. I was the only means of support for our little trio, and although the salary was meager, it paid for food and shelter for the three of us.

It was 8 o'clock in the evening when the pounding on the door startled us. My mother went to the door and opened it.

Three burly men identified themselves to us as representatives from the U.B., known as Urząd Bezpieczeństwa or the Department of Safety-a governing body run by the communist government under the watchful eyes of Russia and firmly ensconced in their new acquisition-the country of Poland.

They explained that they would take me to the police precinct "only to answer a few questions", and that I would be home in no time.

My mother asked if I could eat something as I just got home from work and hadn't eaten all day, but they insisted that this was to be a quick "in and out".

I grabbed my light overcoat, kissed my mother goodbye, and escorted by these three men, left the apartment.

My baby daughter slept unaware, and I didn't want to wake her even for a kiss.

As we stepped out of the apartment lobby, I tried to head to the right, as the police precinct was only a short walk away. The men grabbed me roughly and steered me to the left.

What I saw there made my heart sink and my stomach feel queasy.

It was a paddy wagon.

I was unceremoniously shoved into the wagon and heard the door clang shut behind me.

It would be six months before I would miraculously return to Puławska Street.

CHAPTER II

Siedlce

As I sat in the paddy wagon my thoughts were whirling and my head was spinning. I tried to figure out why I was arrested. It didn't occur to me until much later that my activities during the war in the Polish Home Army led me to this day.

It had been six years since the end of the war and all of us began to piece back some semblance of a normal life. But the communist government spared no effort to round up every soldier, every activist and especially every leader of the resistance in order to effectively eliminate them-whether by a death sentence, life imprisonment or by giving them a one way ticket to Siberia.

After a half hour or so the paddy wagon reached its destination: the intersection of Cyril and Metody Streets. There in the darkness of the night loomed the tall gray buildings of a jail I heard about from my colleagues, and at that sight, my blood ran cold.

Two U.B. guards grabbed me under the arms and threw me out of the paddy wagon. Two more stood on the ground with their rifles pointing at my head.

They led me into the prison, down the stairs and pushed me into a tiny, dark cell.

The cell was just big enough to accommodate a thin straw mattress and a bucket which I assumed served as a toilet.

The door clanged shut. Keys jangled against the lock and a terrible silence descended upon this dismal place, leaving me alone and shaking with the cold and fear of what was to come.

For two days I sat in this freezing hell hole without food or water trying to keep my wits about me. Finally the keys turned in the lock and two guards lifted me up and shoved me out of the door.

As I stepped outside, the guards disappeared and were replaced by two other U.B. officials. This time they were dressed like students from the Polytechnic Institute, even sporting caps with the emblem of that college. There was neither a car nor a wagon waiting for us. This time we were going to the train station because we would mingle in the street with the general public. The disguise of my captors was complete. No one would know that I was a prisoner.

My heart was beating a hundred beats a minute. I was sure that I was being sent to Siberia.

"Goodbye mama, goodbye my baby girl," I whispered quietl". Certain that I would never see them again I let tears well up in my eyes.

In the confusion, fear and sorrow, I forgot that I had not eaten in two days until we neared a stand with bread and assorted buns. My legs almost gave out under me as I inhaled the smell of freshly baked bread and saw a large assortment of croissants, rolls and pastries.

My two disguised guards stopped to buy a couple of buns. One for each of them.

"And one for the lady?" the vendor asked one of the men with a smile.

"My sister doesn't want one," the man replied curtly.

The vendor's face showed momentary confusion and then turned to a stony expression as he realized what he was witnessing.

I don't know how long we rode on the train; it could have been a minute or a day. It felt like all life had been drained from my body.

When we got off, the sign at the train station said "Siedlce".

A car picked us up and shortly afterwards we arrived at the U.B. headquarters.

I had heard about this place-it was known for its interrogations.

The dark hallway inside the building ended in a large iron door. On the other side, a set of stairs led down into the cellar which housed a large cell reserved for male prisoners. In the right and left walls of this very cell I saw doors leading to two smaller cells set aside for single prisoners, and the one on the right side was to be my new home.

It was cold and dark. It spanned no more than 7 feet in length and was about 4 feet wide. On the floor lay a damp straw mattress on which lay a blanket, or rather what was left of a blanket. It was filthy and threadbare.

There was frost on the walls inside my cell, and the metal bucket which was to serve as my toilet was shiny with a thin layer of ice.

Within a half an hour of my arrival I was taken out and pushed in to join eight other prisoners in the larger cell. We were placed with our faces to the wall, our hands behind us, and left to stand there for what seemed like hours.

My teeth were chattering with the cold and with fear of the unknown. As I glanced to the left at my fellow prisoners I noticed that their chins were shaking just like mine. We could not control the shaking of our bodies. It felt like 40 degrees below zero.

The man next to me whispered a question: "Where are you from?"

"Warsaw," I replied.

Immediately a U.B. guard yelled: "Quiet! Quiet or I will smash your face in."

And so, began my life in hell.

Interrogations of the prisoners took place at any time-day or night, it didn't matter. A psychological game was played out when the large bunch of keys would smash against the metal door in the middle of the night waking us out of sleep, heralding an impending interrogation of one or two prisoners.

I could often hear the men through the metal door that separated their cell from mine. They told stories of their interrogations which contained various forms of cruelty. For example, the men would have an entire salty herring shoved down their throat. When later, they begged for a drop of water, it was repeatedly denied. The guards would stomp on the prisoners' bare toes with their heavy boots, pistol whip them, or beat them with their night sticks.

The male prisoners and I communicated regularly through the door that separated my cell from theirs.

One night during our regular whispered conversation the men advised me to get undressed when I went to sleep, and to put my clothing on top of me. Apparently such method kept you warmer.

I tried it. As bizarre as it was, it really did work. Unfortunately, I had to lie very still so the small pieces of what was left of my clothing would not fall off during the night.

Several days passed and I had not been taken out of my cell to be interrogated; I dreaded the uncertainty of what was to come and prayed for it to be over with. Never a staunch Catholic, I now found that prayer calmed and fortified me. It transported me out of that miserable dark hole and gave me strength to believe that a higher power was reachable-that in the end regardless of the outcome, I would be alright.

Every morning I would get a cup of watery, cold coffee substitute and a piece of black bread which had the consistency of clay.

Taking a piece of straw and a thread of what was left of my blanket I rolled the doughy pieces of the bread into little balls and threaded them until I made a rosary. I made a rosary for my mother as I droned on the mantra of the Hail Mary, finding both solace and remembrance as I worked. Then, I made a smaller one, this time for my little daughter.

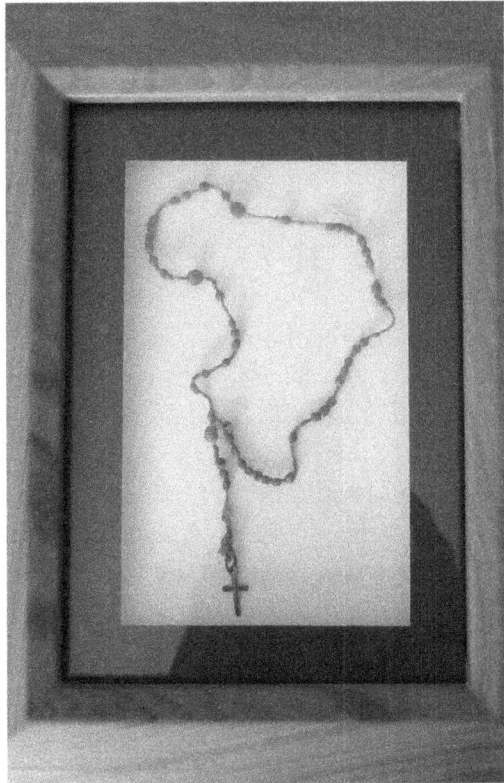

The Rosary made in prison

How were they surviving without my support? Did my mother's heart break at the uncertainty of losing yet another daughter? Did my baby cry and call for me?

I never feared death-not during those awful years of war, and certainly not now. But now I was anxious for my turn at being taken out for that dreaded interrogation, because anything was better that the days and nights alone drowning in uncertainty.

And somewhere, in the midst of my prayers, in the freezing, dark, solitary existence, listening to the other prisoners' screams, waking up several times each night as the guards smashed their keys on the door, somewhere in this nightmare that became my new normal I kept alive that stubborn fragile light of hope for the return to the life I had been forced to leave behind.

CHAPTER III

The Cat and Mouse Game

I slept fitfully lying on that damp straw mattress and dreamt of oak trees with their leaves rustling in the summer wind and their branches hosting a clutch of chirping birds. The sound of keys banging against the lock of the cell woke me out of my reverie. For a moment, in sleepy confusion I could not remember where I was.

The guard did not waste any time in introductions.

"Get dressed!" he yelled into my face. "Hurry up!"

My teeth were chattering as nerves and the freezing temperatures quickly took their toll.

"What's wrong with your face, little girl?" he mocked.

"Can't you feel the cold in here?" I answered boldly.

I regarded him more closely.

He had a pockmarked, doughy face. His lipless mouth intersected it from side to side like a mail slot. Not much taller than me he stood straight up, stretching himself to his full height in an effort to make himself tower above me. I noticed with satisfaction that such effort was completely wasted on his part. He grabbed me by the collar of my blouse ripping it, and pushed me towards the door.

The interrogation room in which we arrived was cold and dim. The clock on the wall showed 2:00 a.m. At the other end of the room stood eight U.B. agents. Each one came up to me and stared into my face. Close. Very close. Immediately after inspecting me thoroughly, one after another walked away and sat down on one of the chairs which lined the wall at the opposite side of the room.

Not one word was spoken.

I stood where they placed me.

The clock ticked and tocked minute after minute. I felt like a cartoon character in suspended animation. The silence screamed in my ears. I lost track of time. In the quiet, the cold and the darkness my head began to swim, and I pitched forward, falling to my knees.

"Make a fire in the stove!" I heard.

For a moment I didn't understand that this was directed towards me. I didn't know if there was a secret to starting a fire in the stove as I had never done such a thing, but I shot back: "Give me matches then. And some paper."

I lit the paper, grateful to be leaning over the warmth. I wanted to stay there and put my freezing hands over the ceramic stove, but my pockmarked friend shoved me back to the place where I originally stood.

The tick tock of the clock once more began to mark off the minutes and the hours of this sick cat and mouse game that was being played out at my expense.

My knees began to buckle and vomit started to rise in my throat as nerves got the best of me, when finally the agents began to get up and one after another began leaving the room.

"Take her back," one growled as he was leaving.

And that command ended this curious "interrogation" at which I wasn't asked a single question.

For the first time since arriving at the interrogation center I was happy to be back in my cell.

I started to pace back and forth like an animal that just eluded its hunters, and even the fact that the cell only accommodated five steps forward and five steps back did not discourage me from my obsessive pacing.

I walked and walked until I wore out holes in my woolen stockings.

Having made the rosary I knew that straw made a good sewing needle. I made a hole in the mattress with my fingernail and pulled out a piece of straw. The thread was easy to pull out of the ancient, thin blanket that was my only source of warmth.

And with such tools, I sewed up the holes in my stockings.

My solitary existence continued. Days turned into nights and one silent week followed another until the brief appearance of a roommate.

Zosia was a young girl from the countryside. She was thrown into my cell for an overnight stay between her internment in the nearby jail and the court in Warsaw where she was being taken next morning for her hearing.

Her crime was giving food and water to the soldiers of the Polish Home Army; a crime which carried with it a sentence of 25 years in jail.

And at that time, 25 years meant exactly that. Not one day earlier.

As the guard pushed her into my cell she fell to her knees and remained kneeling. She sobbed quietly, covering her smudged face in her hands.

I sidled up to her and put my arms around her. She hissed in pain and it was then in the dim light, that I noticed that the back of her shirt was torn and stained with blood. The bloody welts on her back told a horrible story of a beating so savage that she could not bear any touch.

That night she slept on her knees for she could lie neither on her back nor even on her side.

Before we slept, Zosia gave me advice that would take me to another place. I didn't know then that our paths would cross again in a most amazing coincidence.

CHAPTER IV

The Prison

Before Zosia fell into a fitful sleep she told me about her younger sister Ania, who was also taken for interrogation by the U.B. agents.

Upon returning home, Ania told Zosia that the interrogators took her up in a helicopter. While in the air they demanded to know the names of the soldiers whom Zosia provided with water and a bit of food, as well as the names of their leaders. The young girl did not have such information. They pushed her towards the open door of the helicopter and holding her by the hair, threatened to throw her out. When they were finally convinced that she was innocent they landed the helicopter and released her.

"How long have you been here?" Zosia asked.

"One month," I said.

And then she gave me advice that would change everything:

"Pray that they transfer you to the prison not too far from here. You can sleep uninterrupted all night there; they don't interrogate anyone in the middle of the night. And when inspectors come here tell them that, in spite of the rule stating that the prisoners may only be kept here for up to three days, you have been here one full month. I don't trust any of them. I don't know who is clean. They are all communists. But you must a least try to get out of this place."

She was taken away to the prison next morning.

That same morning the guard came to take me for an interrogation. I gathered up my courage which wasn't all that hard to do at this point as anger was boiling inside of me having realized that I was being kept here illegally, and I spewed out the speech which I rehearsed with Zosia that night.

"I know you are not allowed to keep me here more than three days. I have been here for one month. The minute inspection arrives I will tell them what you have done. You won't get away with this!"

As I was talking, or more to the point yelling, out of the corner of my eye I saw one of the agents coming towards me.

"Shut up!" he spat in my face. "Shut your filthy mouth!"

In a split second, I knew.

The butt of his gun hit my head with a sickening thud. White light exploded behind my eyes and a searing pain filled my entire body.

Then everything went dark.

I woke up in my cell. My head throbbed with pain and as I touched it, a bloody clump of hair remained in my hand.

In the morning, the ominous clang of keys against the door of my cell announced the arrival of the guard. "Get up," he scowled. "You're leaving; they are taking you to the prison."

I couldn't believe my ears. It worked. I silently thanked Zosia for her advice.

When we reached the prison, I was thoroughly searched.

I found this quite amusing, as all I had was my purse, and in it a half worn out lipstick and a photo of my brother Wojtek.

"Who's this?" the inspecting agent thrust the photo in my face.

"My brother," I answered.

"Why is he wearing a British military uniform?"

"Because he was fighting for your freedom," I snarled back, putting the emphasis on the word "your". I couldn't help it. My mouth always did get me in trouble. I waited for the inevitable contact of something with my head, a fist a butt of a pistol but none came.

They sent me to my new quarters: cell number 3.

I was no longer alone. At least not at night. My 16 roommates were girls from the Polish Home Army. Their job was to clean the prison, and they worked from daybreak into the evening. I was not allowed to work. I was that "special" prisoner who needed "special privileges" or rather lack of them. They were going to break me. They were sure of it.

During the day, the cell was empty except for bunks made out of wooden boards. These were folded up and secured to the wall, so one could neither sit nor lie down.

A metal bucket stood in the corner and I was given strict instructions that it was for urination only. Should you feel the need to do anything else, you had to wait until 4:00pm, when all 17 of us would be taken to the prison latrine which boasted four metal toilet seats. At that time the female prison guards would stand in front of us yelling to hurry because time was running out and we would be returning to the cell in a few minutes.

4:00pm daily. 17 girls. Four seats. You do the math.

One day I didn't get a chance to use the latrine before they herded us back to the cell. My insides felt ready to explode and my head hurt. I didn't know what to do. Soiling myself felt like the most horrible option. The girls brought me back a piece of paper and gave me these instructions:

"Do it on the paper, roll it up and throw it into the bucket .They won't know," the women advised me.

And that was what I did.

There was no time for shyness. This was no place for humility. It was a place for survival; a place for bonds of friendship and a place which would test the strength of my character to its very core.

CHAPTER V

Prison Life

A couple of times each week we were allowed to go out into the small courtyard where we would walk in a circle for maybe twenty minutes, while a prison guard ensured that our pace did not slow down at any time. It was early March and the weather was still very cold. Snow lay on the ground and one had to be careful to avoid any icy patches which might result in a nasty fall. The prison guard would never allow us to wear any outerwear.

Without a coat or even a jacket, a brisk walk was not only good exercise; it was necessary in order not to feel the freezing cold.

The guard assigned to us was a special breed. She was a prisoner herself, having been incarcerated for spying for the Germans while in Auschwitz. But here they made her a guard, knowing that she would carry out the work with that particular streak of evil which resided in her miserable soul.

"Hurry up you damn cows!" she would scream at us. "Move it, or you'll get this wad of keys across your mouth!"

I wished there would be a special spot in hell for her when the day of reckoning arrived.

Meals in my new home were served twice a day. In the morning, after the girls left for work I received a black coffee, or rather a liquid made from chicory beans that was used as a coffee substitute, and one piece of black bread. In the late afternoon, the lovely entrée was a watery, tasteless "soup" made with mysterious ingredients, the origin of which I do not dare to guess.

One day the door of the cell flew open and a guard threw in something wrapped in a newspaper.

It was a boiled fish.

It was the whole fish with the head, milky eyes, scales and all the innards intact. No one bothered to clean it before they boiled it and wrapped it up for me. I sat on the cold floor and tried to pick off the scales to get at a bit of meat in order to satisfy my twisting hunger.

The loneliness of my existence was almost worse than the hunger. They surely knew what they were doing letting me rot in that cell day after day without a single activity or any one person to open my mouth to. Sometimes my thoughts would swirl in my head like a tornado, and the fear would raise its unwelcome head. At those times I would recite either poems from my childhood or prayers. Sometimes I would sing a song or review mathematical tables. I walked back and forth, recited poetry and talked to the walls; anything not to lose my mind in this dark and damp place of despair.

I celebrated the return of the girls from work each and every evening.

And among the 16 girls who lived in my cell was Zosia who gave me such wonderful advice when we first met at the U.B. interrogation center.

Zosia slept on the straw mattress next to me. She was awaiting trial at the court in Warsaw. If found guilty she would receive a sentence of 25 years in jail.

I wanted to help her, so every night we would huddle together and go over any possible questions that she might be asked at the trial. I played the part of the judge and she of course, herself. These "sessions" lasted three or maybe four months. I had hoped that we covered any surprise questions and that Zosia had enough confidence to answer without faltering.

The day of her trial arrived, and Zosia was swiftly taken away. She never returned to our cell.

One of the features of the cell was a tall ceramic heater which connected our cell to the one on the other side of the wall. It had a small iron door for coal. When lit, the ceramic heater which stretched from floor to the ceiling would keep any room warm and toasty.

Warmth was only a distant dream in the prison, as the heater was never filled with coal nor ever used for heating of the cells. It did however, serve as an occasional means of communication between the prisoners in the adjoining cells. And one day, shortly after the removal of Zosia to the Warsaw court, I heard a tapping on the little iron door of the heater. It was Zosia.

I was anxious to hear how she fared.

"I said everything just the way you taught me," she whispered. "I'm going home tomorrow. I'm free. God bless you and keep you" she continued. "I will never forget what you did for me."

Tears streamed down my face. Her victory was my victory. My happiness for her felt real and palpable. I returned to my damp straw mattress and tried to fall asleep dreaming of one day going home. Just like Zosia did.

Winter turned into spring and our courtside walks became slightly more bearable as the sun increased its intensity. Easter approached and with it a longing for a return to a normal life. An ache to be once again with family and a celebration that was so familiar and joyous.

But I could only dream.

In the meantime, hours dragged on and on in our tiny, crowded cell.

One day the girls smuggled in a few pieces of paper and a pencil from one of the jail offices which they cleaned daily. Out of those scraps I made Tarot cards and in the evenings, to break the monotony and brighten the mood, I told their fortunes.

Several days later a new woman was brought into our cell. Slightly older than the girls in our group, with raggedy clothes and a colourful kerchief covering her hair, she sat in a corner and observed us in silence. I should have known that something was not right, but I gaily continued to tell fortunes and laugh with the girls, momentarily forgetting the grim reality of our surroundings.

I should have listened to my gut.

CHAPTER VI

Solitary

I should have known that this grim, unfriendly, silent woman was placed in our cell to spy on us. And spy she did. She reported my activities to the warden and, once again I was hauled out of the cell by two guards and escorted into a small windowless room.

Four agents appeared in a jovial mood laughing as I walked in.

Unfortunately, this mirth would be at my expense.

"Hey, sister," one of them snorted, "tell us our fortune! Maybe you would like us to get you a black cat? Huh?" With that he brought his face up close to mine.

I could smell vodka and cigarettes on his breath, and I felt my knees weaken. He put his hands on my shoulders and pushed me roughly. I lost my balance and began to fall backwards, but the second man who stood behind me caught me and pushed me forward.

My balance was now nonexistent. I stumbled forward and fell against the hands of to the vodka marinated agent. Again, he pushed me away with some force, and like a ball I bounced back to the man behind me. It was a scene from a school playground with bullies and the bullied, and at that point my tears went away, and the anger rose up in me again.

I broke away and picked up a metal chair that stood nearby. As in a scene from some ridiculous circus, I waved the chair in front of me daring anyone to approach me. For a moment I thought that they might shoot me, but at this point I didn't care. "You goddamn freak!" I screamed. "Did your mother teach you to treat women in this way?" I no longer cared about the possible consequences. I had enough.

Suddenly, the third agent walked up to me and smashed the butt of his rifle against my back. The searing pain took my breath away. For a moment I thought that my back was broken, but I managed to get back up and ignore the throbbing that now took over my entire body.

The three agents began to talk all at once. "Listen sister, we are going to get the information out of you sooner or later. You are going to sing like a canary. You are going to give us names, addresses and shoe sizes of these criminals you worked with. You will spill every name and you will go down with them!" Their venom lit a fire inside me.

"Keep it up you bunch of losers. Keep it up and what I WILL tell in court is how you treated me. How you pushed me around and beat me with the rifle." The vodka stinking agent flew towards me and grabbing my hair pulled my head backwards. "Shut up bitch!" he seethed.

I couldn't help myself - I spat in his face.

He pushed me forward again and I fell on the cold concrete. The other two signalled to him to back off. Things could get ugly now. They grabbed me and dragged me out of the room and down the hall and I realized immediately that we were not going to my cell. Not this time. This time they had a special place for me to cool off in.

It was a cell called "the hole" by the prisoners.

They opened the door of this ominous place and thrust me forward. The thud of the door ended this day's episode.

The "hole" was a room….no, one cannot call it a room. It was literally a hole. It was maybe five feet wide and ten feet long. The only place where you could stand up was immediately by the door because the ceiling sloped down at a steep angle reaching about two feet on the far side. Even sitting was impossible, except tucked against the door through which a tiny stream of light served to prove that there was life on the other side. There was nothing in this so-called room; nothing but a cement floor which would serve as my bed.

For two days and two nights I stood by that door or lay on the concrete floor reciting poems, prayers, and mathematical tables.

I tried not to think about freedom, or my baby, or my mother, for fear that I might lose my mind. I received neither food nor water; no one came to the door and I did not know if this would be the place in which I would die. On the third day the warden opened the door. I slunk back into the sloping ceiling as splintered light blinded my eyes.

My legs, unused to walking shook beneath me. The hunger in my belly suddenly awoke at the possibility of food and water, and supported by the warden, I shuffled towards the luxurious accommodations and the company of the girls in my cell.

CHAPTER VII

Confrontation

It had been almost five months since I was taken from my home.

Five months away from my mom, my baby girl, the life that we so painstakingly attempted to glue together after the apocalyptic days and nights of the war.

I slowly recovered from my stay in solitary and at this point wondered if I will ever see freedom again.

One day a guard came to the cell and ordered me to come with him.

I was going for an interrogation.

Before entering the room, I was told to hide behind the door. Completely baffled, I had no idea what they had up their sleeve this time. After what seemed like hours they led me into the room. Two chairs stood in the middle; one was occupied by Marek, a friend of mine from the Polish Home Army who often spent time in our home during the Soviet Occupation. Our eyes met in complete silence.

And it began.

The interrogator stood over me throwing his gun up in the air and twirling it six centimetres from my face. I was familiar with this threat but did not look away, nor flinch holding his gaze as his fury grew at my insolence.

The questions were directed at Marek and to my horror he spilled the information without blinking an eye.

He told them that we were together in the Underground that he was in the same places as me, etc.

Then the interrogator turned towards me.

"Well now sister, we know all about you. We know who you are, what you have done and where you have been. We do not make mistakes in these matters." His voice rose to a squeal as he spat out the words. "Your friend told us the truth. You are finished. What do you think of that?"

I could smell vodka on his breath as he loomed over me. It made me slightly dizzy but gathering all my courage I spat back: "I don't know this guy; he has mistaken me for someone else. Yes, sometimes I went to the village to buy some cooking oil and something to eat, but I never saw him. I don't know who he is."

Back and forth, back and forth we went as the red-faced interrogator told me that I was lying while I denied everything. I was aware of how badly he wanted to smash that revolver into the back of my head, but there were still protocols. And witnesses. He therefore had to control the urge to beat me to a pulp.

Marek said nothing more and he was not asked any more questions.

They returned me to the cell without the satisfaction of receiving the information they were sure was in their grasp.

One evening the U.B. guards got very drunk. (This was a fairly common occurrence in the prisons at the time.) On this account the charge guards had to place them in a men's cell until they sobered up and, in a domino effect, the male prisoners had to be moved somewhere else.

That "somewhere else" turned out to be the cell next to mine where communication was made possible between two adjoining cells by means of the unused tall ceramic heater with the iron door which you could open quietly and have a conversation with the prisoners next door.

After the doors to the cells were locked, I heard a knock on the door of the heater.

"Who's there?" I whispered.

It was Marek.

"For the love of God, why did you rat me out like that?" I could not hide my fury.

"They beat me so badly; into unconsciousness. I am coughing up blood. I couldn't take any more."

"What sentence did they give you?" I asked.

"They sentenced me to death."

"Well, they can't do any more to you. You heard my testimony. I will have a hearing in the Military court. They will bring you there. Tell them that your testimony was not true and that you were beaten and coerced to tell them what they wanted to hear." It was a long shot, but my life depended on it at this point.

"O.K. I will," he said quietly.*

Seconds later, two U.B. guards stormed into Marek's cell. Having realized that they put him next door to me, they immediately took him away. In a few moments they burst into my cell. "Who were you talking to?" they demanded.

"To nobody. Why, who is there?" I asked wide eyed.

They left grumbling under their breath.

Several weeks later Assistant Warden came into my cell.

"Let's go," he barked.

"Sweet Jesus, I'm going to Siberia," raced through my brain. "Where?" I asked lamely.

"Home."

I froze. No, I was sure that this was just another ruse.

Home. That one word rolled around in my head sounding sweeter than anything I could imagine.

Home. One word that held such joy.

The warden led me to the office where they returned my purse and set me free.

The prisoners with whom I became friends over the six months always said that if and when you are released you must never look back at the gate as you are walking away, or you will come back. Such was the superstition. So, heeding that advice I walked quickly away from the gate and headed towards the train station. Suddenly, I heard someone calling my name. It was the Assistant Warden.

Tears sprung to my eyes and my throat tightened. They did this on purpose. I was already familiar with their psychological games. My knees almost buckled under me, but I stopped in my tracks and waited.

"You didn't take your release forms," he said. "Without them you will be back here in no time." A little smile played on his lips.

I thanked him, took the paper which confirmed my freedom and ran breathlessly to the station to board a train which would bring me home.

Marek was good as his word, and at my trial he recanted his testimony citing brutality and coercion. I met him many years later. He was granted a stay of execution and eventually released.

PART THREE

Story & Musings

Leśny Dar

"I have a surprise for you," he said. "I'm going to take you back in time."

I was visiting Poland, the country of my birth. The year was 1999. Janusz was my childhood friend and later the love of my young life. Our parents met when I was 3 and he was 4 and according to my mom we were engaged by the time I was 5.

I left Poland at the age of 10 and Janusz told me many years later that he cried for days not understanding why they took me away.

Our paths crossed again when I came to Poland in 1970. By now he was engaged and I was a frivolous young Canadian travelling around Europe on my own. Our brief encounter cemented our deep connection, but any plans of togetherness were not to come to fruition. Having completed school, he was scheduled for a compulsory stint in the army. Leaving communist Poland was not an option. For me staying in that country, away from my family and the life to which I was now accustomed was not in the cards either.

We met again in 1997 and spent some time together. Again, timing was not our friend.

That time we had managed to steal a few moments that would remain in my memory forever.

"Where are you taking me?" I asked, curiosity getting the better of me.

"You'll see."

We drove out of the city of Warsaw, leaving the hustle and bustle behind. The roads turned from four lane highways to two lanes and then to country roads. And then I saw the sign. 'Leśny Dar'.

My heart rose into my throat for a few seconds. I looked at him in disbelief. This was the little village at the foot of the Świętokrzyskie Mountains where our parents brought us every summer. For two months we stayed with a farm family in their home. Janusz and his family stayed few houses down. The family we stayed with consisted of a mother, a father and a young boy of 10 years of age or so. The house was a modest hut with no electricity or running water.

There was a well in the back and an outhouse further away. The outhouse terrified me and actually contributed to my obsessive arachnophobia. It was dark in there and every corner was occupied by a veritable cornucopia of spiders and their clever webs. I was terrified to take down my pants and sit on the hole which served as a toilet for fear that those monster spiders which resided behind me would take that very opportunity to explode from their webs onto my bare bum and sink their monster teeth into my nether regions.

The barn was a fantastic playground. Filled with hay to the very top, it served as a sort of Chucky Cheese's recreation center where we could climb up a couple of tiers and throw ourselves into the mountain of hay squealing and giggling until the farmer came in and put an end to the mayhem we caused.

Two cows lived in the shed behind the house, a mother and a daughter. They both had horns and we had to be very careful especially around the younger cow. That one exhibited a certain annoyance with anyone under the age of 30 and often tried to spear us with her still growing horns. The older cow was much, much more laid back, and she's the one I learned to milk-a feat much more difficult than one can imagine. The payoff was a metal cup full of frothy, warm, richly creamy milk that I would gulp down with sheer pleasure.

The farmer had two horses and a wagon that resembled an elongated "V" for carrying hay. Some days he would let us go with him into town. We bounced around the carriage like ping pong balls and yelped with delight as he urged his horses on with soft whistles and light whip of the reins. The farmer's wife baked bread and churned sweet butter from the milk of the two cows. I still remember the smell of baking bread and the long abandoned taste of its slices spread with a thick layer of fresh butter.

At night my grandmother would light the naphthalene lanterns on the night table in our bedroom and I, tucked in and enveloped by down pillows and comforters, would fill my nostrils with that strange familiar scent while she read me a bedtime story.

Days were filled with discovery as Janusz and I wandered off into the fields and forests in search of adventure. We waded barefoot in streams watching the tadpoles as they swam, their long tails wiggling back and forth propelling them on. Sometimes we would catch them and bring them home in a jar wishing to keep them as pets until they turned into full-grown and magic frogs. My grandmother would have none of it and ordered us to release them back to the stream, telling us of the weeping frog mothers and fathers searching for their babies. This horrified us so much that we ran back with our jar and let the tadpoles swim away with visions of their subsequent and joyful family reunions in our heads.

Then there were anthills to observe. The busy traffic around an anthill was a constant source of fascination and discovery. We would never upset their houses. That would not be unfair.

While in the forest, we used the huge rock formations which lived among the trees as shelters from the imagined enemy soldiers, just like we heard the partisans did in the real struggle for survival.

When we got hungry during our day at play, there was plenty to eat. We picked red raspberries, often scratching our arms on the thorny bushes. There were plump blueberries that dyed our fingers indigo and dark juicy plums hanging low on the branches. If we felt particularly energetic we could pull hazelnuts off the trees and break their shells with stones to reach the delicious nuts inside. Gooseberries, lingonberries, even tiny wild strawberries were often on our menu.

Sometimes the overindulgence of these gifts of the land led to an upset tummy and, you guessed it, to a visit of the dreaded spider emporium behind the house.

The carefree days of our childhood summers, filled with wonder, laughter and love passed quickly leaving a sweet memory of sunshine, green fields, fragrant forests and clear, clean streams.

Now, many decades later we stood at the edge of the very forest which we left behind so many years ago. The rock formations still stood silent and proud, keeping the secrets of the days gone by.

I could not find the farmers' house we stayed in. The village looked so much…newer. So much less…pure.

My eyes filled with tears for which I could not find an explanation, and as I turned to Janusz I saw behind him a large brown wooden cross.

"I don't remember that," I whispered.

"It wasn't there when you left," he said.

"Why is it here?"

"You don't know the history of this town?" He seemed surprised.

The only history of this town I knew was my own.

And then he told me the story. During the war, a farmer and his wife took in a family of Jews and hid them in their attic. Upon learning about this, a small troop of Germans came into the village and carried out a terrible warning for the neighbouring villages.

They dragged the Jewish family into the street and shot them in front of the villagers. And then they rounded up the women and the children herding them into a barn. The old men were told to watch as the gates of the barn were bolted and gasoline poured all around. The scent of burning flesh was everywhere and the screams rose with the rancid smoke towards the heavens and onto the troubled face of God.

Then the old men were shot. I stood underneath the cross and wept, the days of my carefree childhood marred by this horror.

Today when I watch television and see children play in sad and troubled places ravaged by conflict and war I feel blessed that in some way I was protected and allowed to run and dream and know that I was safe.

My Mother

Today I wanted to see my mother. No, not the person at Cummer-lodge - not that skeletal, angry shell of a person, but my mother as I knew her all my life.

My mother; the one who could pull me up by my bootstraps and always say: "It will be all right, you'll see. We'll manage." And always we did.

My mother taught me to be strong and brave and fearless and never ever to give up. If a way seemed impossible, one should stand aside, think it through and then approach the problem once again from another angle.

My mother, who could never deny any of my wishes and should I wish for a star in heaven she would surely arrange that, because nothing for her was impossible. Her generosity for her children was as endless as the universe.

Today I wanted to see my mother whose wicked sense of humour brought me to tears of laughter, and whose keen sense of the absurd never ended to amuse me.

Today I wanted to see my mother who would surely find a way for these springtime blues that have a grip on my throat, for she could wipe them away like cobwebs hidden in the corner of the room.

Today I wanted to see my mother to share a cup of tea and daily conversation about the state of the world. That simple conversation always anchored me, comforted me and made me feel that all would surely be well in the end.

Today I felt myself to be a child again and in that childhood reverie, missed my mother with my whole heart and soul.

But in the silence of my room, my tears confirmed that she will never be again the person that I knew. I'm there to make sure her comfort is on-going and to hold her hand for the short time we are together; for the short time I am who I am in her eyes before she drifts off again into the dark and frightening world of her dementia.

Today I wanted my mother back but my outstretched arms found only memories. How cruel the world that brings us together only to recklessly tear us apart.

Puławska 41
March 22,1996

I was in Warsaw with my mother who persuaded me to accompany her in returning to the place of our birth; a place we left in 1959 after subtle but troubling persecution of my mother by the KGB for her activities in the Polish Home Army, which doggedly but in the end futilely resisted the takeover by the communist regime at the end of World War Two.

My cousin Teresa and I were just returning from the theatre when I realized that we were in the neighbourhood where I grew up and just steps away from the house we lived in until our departure for Canada.

"Come, let's take a better look," Teresa steered me towards the low-rise apartment building. As we approached, a weird feeling came over me - like this was a dream - like I would find the scenes of my childhood playing themselves out any minute.

The small garden where I played with the children appeared intact and, as I looked up I saw the windows of our apartment.

Now I was seven years old.

Teresa opened the heavy gate of the building and I walked into the foyer.

The old mailbox was still there, and the stairs down which I fell as a small child leaving me with a tiny scar above my eyebrow stood silent in the waning light of day.

These stairs led up to the first landing; on the left side was our door, and behind it was my grandmother with supper ready and waiting for me.

A feeling of a moment frozen in time gripped my heart and ghosts danced on the stairs and in the hallway.

It was all I could do not to burst into tears.

I had a dream last year, and it was of this moment.

It was dark, just like tonight, and everything I saw in the dream looked the same in real life.

Even the stores across the street were the same. This old apartment stood as a silent testament to my family's life: from the outbreak of war, my grandmother's quiet conspiracy headquarters, my cousin's bravery, my mom's arrest, nocturnal visits of the Gestapo and later, the KGB, the tragedies, joys, births, deaths, laughter, tears, wins and losses, the shadows on my bedroom wall cast by the passing streetcars, the rumble of the communist tanks on the street below, my piano lessons, dark school morning fortified with hot oatmeal, my grandmother's loving hands combing my hair, stroking my face, drying my tears.

It all came back to me like a sea of molten lava and covered me completely. I stood at the bus stop and shook and shook like a leaf. I could not calm down; I could not get a grip-not for a long, long time.

The Shoelace

The June sun baked the city streets with unrelenting heat, but as they passed through the heavy iron gates of the park, a woman and a little girl breathed a sigh of relief.

The tall trees offered a much-needed escape from the sun's rays, and the traffic noises were replaced with the constant chatter of birds, laughter of children and a distant sound of a waterfall.

The woman was tall and slim with chestnut hair and greenest eyes you have ever seen. She wore a white dress with black polka dots, and her waist was cinched with a red belt. By anyone's standards, she was a stunning beauty. The girl of about three or four was dressed also in a white dress with a white and red pinafore. One hand clutched her mother's hand; in the other she held a much loved toy bunny. They headed towards the pond where ducks vied for position with the majestic trumpeter swans, as children threw bits of bread into the water.

The child let go of her mother's hand and headed towards the pond.

"Lalunia, wait a moment!" the mother called. "Your shoelace is undone". She walked up to the girl, bent down and tied up the rebel shoelace. As she got up, she smiled and softly said; "You are my sunshine, baby of mine," as she kissed the child's cheek.

•••••

The June sun baked the city streets with unrelenting heat, but in the park the canopy of leaves offered much needed relief. The birds quarreled in treetops; children ran and played as parents looked on, and squirrels teased the passing dogs into a quick yet futile chase.

Two women strolled down the park lane, their arms entwined.

The older of the two appeared to be well into her eighties, with hair as white as summer clouds, her back slightly bent with ravages of age. She walked slowly, and on her face from time to time appeared a wince of pain. Years of living had left their mark, yet she seemed to be content and free of malice. Suddenly, the young woman stopped and bent down on one knee "Your shoelace is undone" she said as she bent down to tie the rebel lace.

The old woman smiled. "Thank you, Lalunia," she said quietly.

"You are my sunshine mama," I said as I kissed her cheek.

The Two Women

I was the only baby on the ward born with a shock of thick black hair. By the time I was one month old, my mother would tie a big bow on top of my head just to keep the hair from getting matted. By the time I reached the age of seven, my hair reached to the middle of my calves.

I could never wear my hair down, as the slightest movement or a gust of wind would result in nasty tangles; therefore, my hair was always braided. I slept in braids, and every morning ritual included the combing and braiding of my thick tresses. It was my grandmother who was the caretaker of my hair. She was gentle and patient, beginning the combing process at the bottom and slowly working her way higher and higher with the comb, until my entire head was detangled. She would then braid my hair into two braids, each as thick as my arm, and intertwine a ribbon into the bottom of the braid then doubling it up and securing it with a bow behind my ears. The ritual would be followed by hot cream of wheat prepared by our nanny, and a walk to the bus stop where my grandmother would wait until the bus came, and wave to me as I began my journey to the music school which was situated clear across town.

My mother was diametrically opposed in character to my grandmother. As patient and calm as my grandmother was, so was my mother impatient, ebullient and energetic. I dreaded the times when, for whatever reason she would take on the task of combing my hair, because she would grab the comb and begin not at the bottom but at the top of my head, demanding that the tangles yield under her ministrations, and causing me to yelp like a scalded puppy.

As a child of a former underground soldier, which my mother became during the war, I was taught never to whine, complain or otherwise show displeasure at the advent of pain. Even when my aunt Lila, who was a dentist, drilled my teeth with no anaesthetic, and occasionally hit a nerve, even then I could not cry. Crying was for sissies.

My mother did not have a mean bone in her body. She was just raised with incredible discipline doled out by her father. Her father, my grandfather, was an officer in the Polish army at the time when only the elite were allowed to reach that status. In his opinion, children were to be heard and not seen. They would behave in an exemplary manner at all times. They would strip to the waist in the morning and wash with cold water to harden the spirit. They would eat at the table with a knife and fork from the age of three, and never, but never would they be in the company of adults unless invited to play an instrument or sing a song.

My grandmother tried to soften this atmosphere by often breaking his rules, and allowing the children certain liberties when he wasn't looking.

My mother attempted to follow his teachings by imposing similar restrictions and rules upon me. At first, I complied. I curtsied when meeting an adult, I played the piano beautifully, I had good manners at meals and I used "please" and "thank you" with great verve and panache. What happened when I reached teenage years, dear reader is a topic for another time.

But getting back to my grandmother, she was always my calm port in the storm. And if she was my calm port, my mother was a Star Clipper with sails unfurled. Always in a hurry, full of energy and laughter, she would hug and kiss me with such enthusiasm that my eyes would water. My grandmother, on the other hand, would stroke my hair gently and kiss me with calm tenderness.

The two women in my life, as different as they were, shared three incredible characteristics: courage, strength of survival and the knowledge that one must never give up.

My grandmother was a child of 16 when she married her first husband, a man 20 years her senior. She bore him three children: two girls and one boy. Her life was full of privilege and comfort. There were estates and servants to see to her every need. Years later, after her first husband's death, she married my grandfather and had two more children, a boy and the youngest child, a girl, who later became my mother.

The halcyon years of her youth would soon come crashing down, as war made its unwelcome presence. Her two older daughters, who were already married with children of their own, were sent to a concentration camp in Oświęcim, renamed Auschwitz by the Germans.

(Many years later, as we made our life in Canada, we heard that her oldest boy, my uncle Władek, while travelling on business was one of the unfortunate passengers on a civilian plane that was shot down over the Sinai desert by the Israeli air force.)

After the horror and crushing grief of her daughters' deaths, my grandmother stepped up to the plate to lose herself in conspiracy, the headquarters of which were in the wartime apartment located ironically an few hundred feet from a German post. It's always safest where it is thought to be insanely unsafe, I learned later.

Because of this unstable and dangerous situation, my grandmother decided to send my mother to the care of a friend of hers who was a commander in the Polish underground. It was a hard decision for her, but a potential life saver for my mother.

There, in the forest, life began for my 16 year old mother. Nothing could have prepared her for what was in store. No one could have warned her of the cold, the damp, the fear, the blood, the death, the ambushes, the night relocations, the lice, the hunger, the longing for even a tiny smattering of a normal life. She learned to walk while asleep, with her hand hooked into the belt of the soldier in front of her. She learned to take apart, clean and put together a rifle which she also learned to use.

She learned to dip a stick in the fire, and with its glowing tip to burn the lice off the backs of her compatriots. She learned that because you have become good friends with one boy, you must put those feelings aside when you find him shot with his eyes gouged out. She learned about the swift forest justice as a soldier that was found to be a spy for the Germans was brought back to camp and unceremoniously shot in the back of the head. She learned that just because you found a nice comfy ditch to sleep in didn't mean that you won't wake up covered in mud and water as the rains come in.

And so passed her teenage years. No prom dresses, no makeup lessons, no hand-holding in a darkened movie theater, no sodas with girlfriends in a nearby café, no walks in a park on a sunny spring day. No Christmas around the family table, or birthday cakes. Not even the dreaded school exams.

Yet there were many more trials to follow.

As a soldier in what is now called "The Home Army", my mother with her colleagues continued to oppose the Russians as they came in to "save us" from the Germans. This branded her as an enemy of the state. (Incidentally, after the fall of Communism, the Polish Home Army is now touted as heroes, an honour which came much too late for a great number of the soldiers.) Shipped out to Siberia, she escaped from the convoy. Taken to the wall by Russians to be executed, she was spared at the last minute. Taken out of our home by the SB in the middle of the night in 1951 and thrown into horrendous surroundings of a prison for 6 months, she managed to pull of another miracle and be released. And somehow, within all that she endured, my mother adopted an attitude that was a combination of courage, intolerance for anything unjust, belief in a better tomorrow as well as disdain for any self-pity.

And somewhere between the role model provided to me by two of these women, I tried to find my balance in life.

It has not always been easy.

Wielka Street

Krysia or "Kitty" was the youngest of five children of Zofja, a wonderful and noble Catholic woman born into the privileged class of prewar Poland. There were servants and estates to be run and the gentle Zofja was beloved by her friends as well as the servants whom she treated as her own family. Never having to cook or clean she was one of the many women whom one would assume to be spoiled and unable to fend for herself.

In 1939 the life she knew came to an abrupt and horrible end when Poland was invaded by the Germans, and shortly afterwards by its "friends" the Russians.

Instead of shrinking away from the scene around her, she and her two eldest daughters, Irena and Janina entered into conspiracy, eventually setting up their house situated several miles from the city of Warsaw as a main hub for the falsifying of passports for those in need, and the storage and distribution of weapons.

Irena's husband was taken away and executed by the Germans soon after the onset of the war in what was known as the Außerordentliche Befriedungsaktion, or Extraordinary Operation of Pacification, a Nazi German campaign aimed to eliminate the intellectuals and the upper classes of the Polish people and of Polish nationhood.*

Janina's husband was away fighting in the forests and the villages against the oppressor.

The quiet town of Zielonka was a perfect camouflage for the work being done by Zofja, Irena, Janina and the many volunteers who worked around the clock to save lives and put a cog in the deadly machine of the Nazi occupation.

The mass murder of Polish leaders, politicians, artists, aristocrats, the intelligentsia, and people suspected of potential anti-Nazi activity was seen as a pre-emptive measure to keep the Polish resistance scattered and to prevent the Poles from revolting during the planned German invasion of France. The anti-Polish campaign was prepared by Hans Frank, the commander of the General Government, and was also discussed with Soviet officials during a series of secretive Gestapo-NKVD Conferences

Ref: Noakes and Pridham, Nazism: A History in Documents, p. 965.

In a horrible turn of events while Kitty and her mom were in Warsaw, the Germans, tipped off about the activities in the town of Zielonka, arrested the two women and their three children and took them to Pawiak, a dreaded Warsaw prison. From there, the women were transported to Auschwitz where they eventually died. The children were spared by the quick thinking of Zofja's eldest son who paid an undisclosed amount of money to have them released from Pawiak prison before the transport to Auschwitz. The children were told to walk away from the prison gates and not look back. Someone would come and get them. Irena's two children, a boy of 15 and a girl of 13, bravely pushed forward, but little 6-year-old Adam, Janina's son, sobbed and called for his mom.

The news of her daughters' internment shook Zofja to the core. She and the youngest Kitty were not safe; they were a target now. They were marked for death.

Connections were made and Zofja, through a co-conspirator, managed to find a safe place for her and Kitty in an abandoned apartment building on Wielka Street in Warsaw. This building, occupied by Jewish Poles before the war, now sat abandoned, as the Jews of Warsaw were rounded up and herded into a walled off area--the Jewish Ghetto.

The apartment was completely empty except for two single beds, but it was the last place anyone would look for these two wanted women. It was safe by virtue of its location.

The large concrete balcony offered Kitty a clear view of the Jewish Ghetto, and she could see all the activity, all the suffering and all the horror as it unfolded. She could also see that every day in the wall of the Ghetto appeared an opening where the bricks were removed. People appeared with produce and goods of all sorts. Serious bartering was taking place, and the ghetto hummed with activity.

Inside the Ghetto, a young man of about twenty or so caught Kitty's eye. At the young age of 18, caught in this awful war, she was unable to forge normal friendships and relationships. And so, between the balcony and the wall, the two struck up a friendship.

He told her that he was a sentry. His job was to watch out for the Germans as the bartering and exchange of goods took place. So every day she would come out on the balcony and they would talk as he kept a watchful eye on the surroundings.

One cloudy morning as the hole in the Ghetto wall buzzed with activity and Kitty and the young man chatted, she turned her head to see from her vantage point high on the balcony, several German soldiers hunched down, their rifles drawn and ready approaching the Ghetto. Someone must have tipped them off.

Frightened that they might spot her, she slunk as far back on the balcony as she could, nevertheless gesticulating madly to her sentry friend below with a silent charade showing him drawn guns.

He understood immediately. Within seconds, the hole in the wall disappeared and so did all the people on either side of it.

The Germans arrived to find absolutely nothing going on. They left without an incident, their rifles slung on their backs.

The next day, the young sentry beckoned for Kitty to come down to the Ghetto wall. She declined, telling him that she was afraid.

He insisted.

Drawing up her courage, she ran downstairs and sidled up to the hole in the brick wall of the Ghetto. And through it, he slid a small box and a note.

She ran upstairs breathless and hopeful that she was not seen. In the box were wonderful, fragrant, baked cookies and the note said: "With heartfelt thanks for saving the lives of Jewish workers of the Ghetto."

Shortly afterwards, the Ghetto Uprising drew out the fury of the Germans who emptied it of its many inhabitants.

The Warsaw Uprising followed. Kitty and he mother had to flee the apartment, leaving behind the few belongings that they managed to keep, including the little box in which Kitty kept the note from the Jewish people of the Ghetto.

It was lost, or stolen, or destroyed. She would never know.

Years later, she would say to me: "That note was the most wonderful gift I have ever received, because if you can save even one human life you have not lived in vain."

Kitty was- is my mother; Zofja, my wonderful grandmother. I owe them a debt of gratitude for instilling in me courage, perseverance, and respect for life.

Krystyna with her mother Zofja.

Krystyna with Pope John Paul ll

Clockwise from the top, Zofja, Krystyna, Margaret, and her daughter Janina.

Krystyna with Prince Charles

*Jerzy Stefanowski "Habdank" and Krystyna in front of a
Polish partisan's grave.*

Jacek, Margaret, Krystyna and Andrew

Krystyna